EMPOWERMENT EVALUATION IN THE

DIGITAL VILLAGES

EMPOWERMENT EVALUATION IN THE DIGITAL VILLAGES

Hewlett-Packard's $15 Million
Race Toward Social Justice

DAVID M. FETTERMAN

STANFORD BUSINESS BOOKS

An Imprint of Stanford University Press
Stanford, California

Stanford University Press
Stanford, California

Special discounts for bulk quantities of Stanford Business Books are available
to corporations, professional associations, and other organizations. For details
and discount information, contact the special sales department of Stanford
University Press. Tel: (650) 736-1782, Fax: (650) 736-1784

Printed in the United States of America on acid-free, archival-quality paper

Library of Congress Cataloging-in-Publication Data

Fetterman, David M., author.
  Empowerment evaluation in the digital villages : Hewlett-Packard's $15
million race toward social justice / David M. Fetterman.
    pages   cm
  Includes bibliographical references and index.
  ISBN 978-0-8047-8111-4 (alk. paper)—ISBN 978-0-8047-8112-1 (pbk. : alk.
paper)
  1. Digital divide—United States—Case studies. 2. Social justice—United
States—Case studies. 3. Community development—United States—
Evaluation—Case studies. 4. Evaluation research (Social action programs)—
United States—Case studies. 5. Hewlett-Packard Company. I. Title.
  HN90.I56.F48   2012
  303.48'33—dc23   2012016180

Typeset by Westchester Book Composition in Minion, 10.5/15

This book is dedicated to my son, David Mark Fetterman II, who walks into a room and fills it with energy, excitement, and happiness. We play the "I love you game" in the car, my study, the beach, wherever we are. He begins, "I love you from the earth to the moon." I follow him with, "From the bottom of the ocean to the highest stars in the sky." It goes on forever, much like our love for this little man.

David, you have a big heart and a generous spirit. I write this book in hope that it helps readers to create a better world—for you, for our family, and for communities everywhere.

CONTENTS

ACKNOWLEDGMENTS

I am indebted to Hewlett-Packard for their commitment to this ambitious project, their trust in local community-based change efforts, and their wisdom to select an evaluation approach, in this case empowerment evaluation, that is in alignment with their values and the communities' interests. Specific thanks are extended to Carly Fiorina, HP Chairman and CEO at the time; Debra Dunn, Senior Vice President, HP Corporate Affairs; and Bess Stephens, Vice President and Director, HP Philanthropy & Education.

I also extend my thanks to my colleagues at Stanford University, particularly at the Haas Center for Public Service. They helped negotiate and broker this arrangement. Nadine Cruz, the former director, was an invaluable asset in this regard. Carilee Pang and Thomas Siegel were instrumental in arranging many of the community sessions, recording the dialogue, and synthesizing what we learned at every stage.

Richard Shavelson, Dean of the School of Education, generously supported my Policy Analysis and Evaluation Program and required evaluation practicum during this period and offered numerous suggestions and recommendations that were applied to the project.

Digital Village members made this dream a reality. This book would not have been possible if not for their dedication, commitment, and hard work. Of special note, I would like to thank Tribal Digital Village members Denis Turner, executive director of the Southern California Tribal Chairmen's Association; Jack Ward, TDV manager; and Linda Locklear, Professor at Palomar College. In addition, East Palo Alto Digital Village members who provided invaluable insight into the effort included Faye McNair-Knox, Sharon Williams, Regina Thompson, Rebecca Mathews, Sue Allen, Stewart Hyland, and Omowale

Satterwhite. Baltimore Digital Village members who made significant contributions to the collaboration included Shelonda Stokes, Tisha Edwards, and Diane Bell. Helpful HP Digital Village liaisons included Janiece Evans-Page, Camilla Nelson, Scott Bossinger, and Joann Strathmeyer.

Insightful comments from colleagues, particularly Stewart Donaldson, Lennise Baptiste, and Margo Beth Fleming, helped shape and focus my eyes on the most pertinent points to be told in this story about corporate philanthropy, academic expertise, and a community-based social justice initiative.

Abraham Wandersman, my collaborator and longtime friend, helped me crystallize my vision of empowerment evaluation, for which I will be eternally grateful.

Excursions of this nature require a tremendous amount of time, attention, and thought. Time disappears for the writer, but not for those around you. I was fortunate to have the support and understanding of my family, and my wife Summer in particular, as I immersed myself into the process of telling this story.

EMPOWERMENT EVALUATION IN THE

DIGITAL VILLAGES

1 THE FUEL:

THE DESIRE FOR A BETTER LIFE

Desire is the key to motivation, but it's the determination
and commitment to an unrelenting pursuit of your goal —a
commitment to excellence—that will enable you to attain
the success you seek.
—Mario Andretti

People, however evolved, rely on food to function. It is actually ironic how simple, almost archaic, our bodily systems function. We do not beam nutrients into our blood vessels, muscles, and tissues. Our nutrients come from simple and complex sugars, carbohydrates, proteins, and of course water. However, the diet for comprehensive community change[1] is more complex than our normal menu of daily calories. Just as a race car needs a higher-octane fuel than a streetcar, a human being in a race against time and extraordinary odds needs to be supplied by a much richer mixture. Desire is the fuel of choice that drives any successful community change initiative.

People have to want to see things get better for themselves, for their families, and for their community. It is that insatiable thirst for a better life that sustains the often Herculean effort required to transform the world around us. It is a challenge in part because of the natural forces of inertia that reinforce the status quo. It is Herculean because many of the people in this story began from a starting point that few of us can imagine. Many of the communities, such as tribes brought to the brink of extinction, have been disempowered for generations.[2] Alcohol and drug abuse, domestic violence, and unemployment all loom in the background of these stories. But this is not another story about blaming the victim,[3] victimization, or any of those stigmatizing tales. This is a story of resilience,[4] the single-minded pursuit of a goal, and an unrelenting commitment to excellence. It is also a story about people learning to help themselves and the often untold story about people helping people to help themselves. But before we get too far ahead of ourselves, let us begin with what this story is about, why it was written, and what you might hope to get out of it.

WHAT THIS BOOK IS ABOUT

This book is about helping to navigate a $15 million Hewlett-Packard venture called the Digital Village. It was a large-scale, community-based initiative,[5] funded at a level designed to make a difference. It was a successful effort. It helped people bridge the digital divide.[6] This venture involved a partnership between Hewlett-Packard, Stanford University, and three Digital Villages, ethnically diverse communities of color throughout the United States.

WHY I HAVE WRITTEN THIS BOOK

I have written this book to share what people can accomplish on their own when given the opportunity and the right tools and resources. The potential of the most disenfranchised—the people we have left behind—is enormous. However, converting potential into productivity can't be left to chance. If success is largely attributable to an accumulation of opportunities that are acted on at successive stages, as Malcolm Gladwell (2008) suggests, the opposite also holds true. Denying opportunities over time is cumulative and potentially devastating, not only to the individual but to entire communities. The story that is about to unfold demonstrates how it is possible to break free from a negative spiral. It describes how a "safe track" that is designed to cultivate educated guesses, risk taking, and seizing opportunities can transform society.

I have also shared this story to highlight the power of the engine behind this tale: "empowerment evaluation."[7] It is logical that if you want to turn society around 180 degrees, you have to use an equally radical or different set of driving instructions than the ones we have used in the past. Empowerment evaluation is an approach that is at least a standard deviation away from the status quo. This brand of evaluation focuses on building capacity and improving communities. It has been successful internationally[8] because it is simple—only three steps—and because it works. It is a radically different view of evaluation. In fact, many believe it stands evaluation on its head. The community is in charge of the evaluation, instead of the individual expert or evaluator. The speed and direction of the evaluation are determined and controlled by the community. The empowerment evaluator is a coach, a facilitator, and a mentor. Evaluators keep the project rigorous, on track, and under control.

However, empowerment evaluators do not control the evaluation—the evaluation remains in the hands of those who have a stake in the community long after any individual project has come and gone.

Finally, I have written this book to demonstrate the power of corporate philanthropy,[9] academic prowess, and community empowerment. When these societal forces converge, they can forge a team that is powerful enough to help people help themselves—and in this case, that is exactly what Hewlett-Packard, Stanford University, and three communities of color accomplished. However, we cannot expect people to "pull themselves up by their bootstraps" without assistance or guidance. That would be an abdication of responsibility. Instead, a collaboration, a partnership, or even a marriage is necessary—a plan that is designed for the "long haul" and that produces real, measurable outcomes. It is my hope that the example laid out in this book can serve as a model for those committed to social change and social justice. Ideally, it can also serve to revitalize the triumvirate of philanthropic, academic, and community forces throughout the United States and the world. The time is right to reassemble this socially conscious team to address new challenges on the social horizon.

WHO I HOPE WILL READ THIS BOOK

At the broadest level, this book was written for citizens who are committed to constructive, progressive social change. These include community organizers and activists, social workers, clergy, city planners, foundation officers, and politicians. It was also written to help individual concerned citizens in communities throughout the world who wish to make a difference. For many, this book will serve as a blueprint for change. Others will simply use it as a guide, or set of general directions, to be adapted to their own local environment. In any case, these readers are some of the most powerful change agents in society. They are rooted in and invested in the community. They understand the value of selecting an authentic process and the moral and economic imperative of producing results. They are also not interested in reinventing the wheel. This book saves time and precious resources by providing a model of success.

I have also written this book for my academic colleagues, particularly evaluators, educators, and health-care providers. They were the first to see the power of the empowerment approach and the synergy generated by combining the forces of corporate philanthropy, academia, and community. They were the first to accept the proposition that evaluation could be used as a tool to help people help themselves by offering local control, rigor, honesty, and effectiveness—a rare combination. This book builds on their knowledge of the literature by providing a large-scale case example. It provides the theory, concepts, principles, and even a set of step-by-step instructions in the guise of a story—three stories, actually—about socially constructed change.

Finally, this book was written for the skeptic who no longer believes that social change is possible, nor that it can be orchestrated by people in their own communities. This example of a social experiment that worked was written to remind those who have lost their optimism, hope, and faith in the future what is possible and within their reach. As Mark Twain wrote: "Few things are harder to put up with than the annoyance of a good example."[10]

WHAT READERS STAND TO GAIN

This book provides the reader with an insight into the power of community to harness the energy within itself, turn itself around, and be its own driving force into the future. These stories are expressions of self-determination,[11] self-efficacy,[12] and local control. They are the powerful forces, often dormant, in a community. However, they are predictably poised to help a community leap forward. They are the invisible forces standing a little ahead of the curve waiting to be transformed into action in any community. Empowerment evaluation is simply one of many tools to harness and to redirect social energy.

On a practical level, reading these stories and understanding empowerment evaluation is like learning to drive a car around a curve. Normally you learn to start steering into the curve far in advance of the bend in the road. You are anticipating it. This process is similar to the way normal incremental change happens in a community. It is driving with an eye ahead of where you are going. However, in any comprehensive community initiative designed to change the social fabric of a community, the pace is accelerated. You are no longer just driving to get from one destination to another, you are racing and racing rules apply.

When you race you learn to drive the driver's line[13] (the straightest path from one point to another), which means using every inch of the road. You learn to aim for the apex or the center of the turn in order to maximize your speed, minimize the distance you travel, and produce the fastest exit speed. Empowerment evaluation helps a community to anticipate and to embrace the power behind the curve. It helps them to position themselves so that they remain on the driver's line on the other side of the curve, even though they can't see the other side as they approach it. The curve, from a social reform perspective, is simply a series of obstacles reframed and transformed into opportunities. Every group faces them as they forge a new future together. Empowerment evaluation helps people to maximize the power of group problem solving and transform this power into strategies and solutions that catapult the community into the future.

Failure to anticipate the curve and to adjust for it before you enter the curve typically results in overcorrection, which pushes the social agenda off its track. The same holds true for comprehensive community initiatives and evaluation. Large-scale change is like building a highway while racing on it. A conceptual lens such as empowerment evaluation can help keep things in focus along the way. Empowerment evaluation enables the community to steer in the right direction and to stay on course even when there are no street signs or signals because *community members* build the road and *they* draw the conceptual map to *their* desired destination.

The stories about these Digital Villages can help readers learn how to look ahead of the curve. They provide a peek into the future and the future is more, not less, local control. People in communities around the world have been mistreated or exploited by politicians, physicians, social scientists, and external experts. The Tuskegee syphilis experiment[14] is a case in point. African Americans were used as human guinea pigs. They were diagnosed and left untreated by physicians in order to study the natural history of the disease. This kind of treatment by external experts explains in large part the low participation of African Americans in clinical trials, organ donation efforts, and routine preventive care. People have good reason to be skeptical about outsiders. More and more, they have come to trust themselves as constructive agents of social change in their own communities.

The Digital Villages have embraced the popularized "glocalization" concept: think globally, act locally (Wellman, 2002). Subway does not have beef in its stores in India, and McDonald's has a Teriyaki McBurger with Seaweed Shaker Fries in Japan. Likewise, the Digital Villages learned to listen to members of their communities and to shape their services accordingly to meet their varying needs. The results for one Digital Village ranged from the noble task of preserving native languages and cultural traditions on the reservation to the economically pragmatic step of creating the Tribal Print Source (formerly the Hi Rez [high-resolution] printing service).[15]

Once a community has even a taste of what it feels like to effect change and improve itself, especially on a grand scale, there is no going back. The feeling of control over a community's life is intoxicating as it demonstrates its self-efficacy. It also has a force all its own, commanding the attention of people from all walks of life. Human beings are social animals. They are drawn to the collective will, particularly when it is successful, productive, and in their self-interest. This small core of individuals becomes the catalyst for change, attracting neighbors and friends who enlist in the campaign for social change.

This story also reminds us of what we can do to change our own world, once freed from the self-imposed slavery of antiquated ways of thinking and conceptualizing the boundaries of our universe. The story of Hewlett-Packard, Stanford, and the local communities of color working together can renew our faith in people as responsible agents working together for the common good. This story demonstrates how individual self-interest and the community's larger interests can converge to produce radically successful outcomes.

Readers may also gain a less jaundiced view of corporate America and academia as they turn each page. Both are in dire need of reinventing or at least repackaging themselves, and this story provides a credible portrait of their efforts to reform and refocus their "eyes on the prize."[16] Discussing problems and airing disagreements and conflicts as we work to facilitate local capacity provides a more realistic, authentic, and replicable model of social intervention and change. It also provides a more nuanced, less predictable view of these powerful agents in action.

Finally, evaluators will be able to see another powerful example of what happens when you turn evaluation on its head. Many evaluators have long held the belief that only they can conduct evaluations. They are the only ones who can be objective, honest, critical, and accurate. However, as this and many other examples confirm, that view is not only wrong, it is misguided and no longer productive.

Evaluations are not neutral or free from political or economic influences.[17] Moreover, people (given guidance and appropriate tools) are typically more critical of their own organizations because they have to live with them and they want them to work. Similarly, empowerment evaluators who are sympathetic toward a certain type of program are typically more critical because they believe in the concept or theory behind a program and want them to serve the intended purpose.

Much knowledge is lost in evaluation because it resides in a report that is sitting on a shelf and gathering dust. These reports are read by a few and used by no one. Empowerment evaluation findings are used routinely to inform decision making. People have a sense of ownership when they are responsible for their own evaluations and are thus more likely to use the findings and to follow the recommendations—because they are theirs.

For those who have already seen the power of this approach, this book becomes another useful tool and case example to illuminate and to refine their own work. It provides the tools of the trade, maps of the minefields, and answers to classic questions. This book also provides evaluators with a new way of looking at the relationship between evaluation and social change.

WHAT LIES AHEAD

The story begins in Chapter 2 with a description of the sponsor and the crew, specifically Hewlett-Packard and Stanford University. They are long-term partners with the resources, commitment, and common purpose that provide the context for this digital initiative.

Chapter 3 provides the reader with a description of the drivers in this race, the three Digital Villages. Unlike many stories, this one begins with the end—a picture of the Digital Village outcomes and accomplishments. The magnitude of their accomplishments underscores why it is important to describe how this initiative transpired so that it might be replicated, exported, and adapted in other communities. It also makes this large-scale, community-wide initiative more meaningful, relevant, and understandable because it describes real people in real-world settings.

Empowerment evaluation, the conceptual engine that drives this social intervention, is presented in Chapter 4. This chapter defines the approach and discusses the theories and concepts guiding this type of evaluation. It also describes the simple three-step process used by the Digital Villages to monitor and to assess their own performance including (1) establishing their mission, (2) taking stock of their performance, and (3) planning for the future in order to implement the intervention and improve program performance. This chapter also highlights the role of the "critical friend" who helps to facilitate the effort yet respects community control. The empowerment evaluation approach was purposefully selected because it aligned with the philosophy and ethos of the sponsor and the Digital Village communities.

Chapter 5 places everyone at the starting line. This is where the Digital Villages established their mission and clarified their community values. Hewlett-Packard and Stanford (in the form of the empowerment evaluators) stood right by their side, helping them take their first steps on this road toward social change and transformation.

Chapter 6 highlights the "taking stock" step, which is much like a pit stop in a race. It is a rapid appraisal process in which the Digital Villages work like a well-oiled machine, inspecting their program (their vehicle for social change), making necessary repairs, and recording the dashboard of program indicators at every stop. Without this step, there would be no beginning and no ending. In addition, there would be no way for the Digital Villages to monitor their performance while in the race.

Chapter 7 places the Digital Villages back on track as they plan for the future and implement their intervention strategies. This step, in which the Digital Villages establish their goals and identify the strategies they plan to implement in order to accomplish their goals, is called "planning for the future." It is also the step in which they come up with credible evidence to determine if their strategies are working.

Chapter 8, the finish line, measures change over time. It depends on measurements recorded at every evaluation pit stop in the race, particularly during the first and last pit stops. This chapter compares where each Digital Village started with where it ended. It is the final program implementation lap of the race. It is a story replete with successes and missteps all along the way.

This chapter provides some insight into the different adaptations required to accommodate the three Digital Village community contexts and at the same time emphasizes the similarities they share that help to unite them.

Chapter 9 is a celebration of the real winners in this race: the Digital Village communities. It brings one of the most important elements in the story from the background to the foreground: capacity building. It is at the heart of HP's mission and the cornerstone of the Digital Villages' efforts. It is also one of the guiding principles of empowerment evaluation. Building capacity is what sustainability is all about. Skills and competencies acquired in the process of building the Digital Village can be used in other initiatives. Capacity building can help keep a community productive and on track well into the future.

Chapter 10 concludes this story of the Digital Villages. It is a reflective piece, asking the simple question: What did we learn about this race to social justice? It highlights what worked in this social experiment and what was required to make it work. It also discusses some of the challenges encountered in an open and candid manner. Hewlett-Packard, the Digital Villages, and the empowerment evaluators share lessons learned. The topics that emerged from this story are not your typical list of mechanistic problems and solutions. They range from simple human communication to the more complex phenomenon of organizational hubris.

This Digital Village story contributes to our growing body of knowledge about community-based social change. As one of many success stories being told around the world about capacity building, local control, and investing in the future, it is part of a cumulative knowledge base being used to drive the spirit of debate in the body politic. This story is also part of a larger commitment to revitalize our communities and to rejuvenate our nation.

2 THE SPONSOR AND THE CREW: HEWLETT-PACKARD AND STANFORD UNIVERSITY

This is the biggest race of the year, Daytona. This is the one that
everybody wants to be at, this is the one every sponsor wants to be
involved in.
—Paul Tracy

The Digital Village sponsor (Hewlett-Packard) and the crew (Stanford University) invested their time and energy in the Digital Villages because they believed they could help them accomplish their goals and objectives—to cross the finish line with demonstrable results and outcomes. The investment was significant—$15 million—and the Digital Villages had the best chance in town to have a significant social return on investment.[1] A seasoned sponsor and a skilled crew could see that it was a once-in-a-decade project that had the potential of breaking all the records.

HEWLETT-PACKARD AND STANFORD UNIVERSITY: HOW THEY CAME TOGETHER TO SUPPORT THE DIGITAL VILLAGE PROJECT

Hewlett-Packard and Stanford University have a long history together. Hewlett and Packard were engineering classmates at Stanford University. Their backyard garage where they started their business is part of the Silicon Valley lore. HP and its innovative management policies have been a model, or prototype, for many Valley start-ups[2] HP's open door policy encouraged employees to speak to management as issues and concerns arose, not unlike Google's management style (Ryssdal, 2009; Schmidt, 2007).[3] According to former Google CEO Eric Schmidt (in Mubbisher, 2011),

> We encourage dissent, we encourage large group conversation, we encourage there to be somebody who's opposed to the decision, and we work very, very hard to be not hierarchical in the way that decisions are made. Often if we can get a decision, we get the best decision if we have two decision makers, not one. We never make decisions in private; we always do them right in front of everybody.

This view is similar to those of Drucker (2002) on managing modern knowledge workers who are viewed as an asset[4] rather than a cost. HP embodied this way of thinking. HP employees were placed in cubicles and executives had offices without doors, encouraging an open flow of communication. This management style and atmosphere called the "HP Way,"[5] coupled with the innovation of profit sharing, attracted East Coast technology experts.

Stanford is equally well known.[6] It is a top Tier 1 research university.[7] Admission is highly selective. Stanford recently received more applications than any other university in the United States, including Harvard.[8] Stanford alumni have consistently reached the highest positions in business, education, legal, medical, and government sectors.[9] They have received the highest honors in their respective professions. They have also been generous in their gratitude by rewarding Stanford for the training they received.

Hewlett and Packard followed in this tradition. In the process of fueling the growth of Silicon Valley, Hewlett and Packard were able to find many places for Stanford graduates to work without having to see them shipped back east. Over the years, their individual generosity toward Stanford has been extraordinary. "Packard and Hewlett made personal donations of more than $300 million to Stanford University" (Stanford University News Service, 1996). The relationship has been and continues to be reciprocal. Hewlett-Packard readily calls on Stanford to provide training and expertise, as the need arises, in areas that have ranged from early distance learning engineering programs to evaluation services.

The Digital Village was one more of those mutually beneficial opportunities. Hewlett-Packard was about to embark on an ambitious project—to bridge the digital divide. They wanted to help low-income, disenfranchised communities of color to access the Internet and to productively use digital cameras, computers, scanners, and printers. Through an infusion of technology and training, they wanted to stimulate the growth and development of small businesses in ethnically diverse communities of color throughout the United States.

Hewlett-Packard had a task to accomplish—to help Digital Village partners credibly and honestly monitor their progress and assess their performance. They knew they needed formative corrective feedback to build their programs and to improve their performance. They also knew that everyone wanted to know what the summative judgment would be at the end of the day. Did the

Digital Villages accomplish their objectives? HP wanted to learn from this experience in order to determine whether they should replicate the social experiment. More precisely, they wanted to know how to duplicate their successes while they learned from their mistakes in this pilot program.

They were confident about their ability to deliver the equipment and technical training. However, like any intelligent company, they knew what they did not know—how to measure a social, rather than an engineering, experiment. They wanted answers to a few simple questions:

- How do you know if you have accomplished what you set out to do?
- How do you know if it made a difference?
- How do you do these things while keeping the program where it belongs—in the hands of the people living in their own communities?

Finding answers to questions such as these is what evaluators do all the time, and HP knew that they could find this expertise and these competencies at Stanford.

At the time, I was working on a similar digitally oriented project in East Palo Alto funded by a local foundation. They were not satisfied with the community's progress, so they "took the project back" from the community and in essence fired everyone. One community member said, "It felt like a bunch of rich white educated folks slapping a lot of us Black folks around again." The project was micromanaged[10] to death by the local foundation, and anyone who had a financial alternative and who was not already dismissed backed away from the project. People in the community were demoralized. They were trusted to take on major responsibilities, only to have them publically snatched away from them. Once again, they were being told how they did not measure up. Those in power made the rules, broke the rules, and changed the rules in the middle of the game. They had the money and they called the shots. The project goals and objectives were accomplished. The funder did an excellent job in completing the project, but nothing lasted. Each of the major pieces of the project fell apart when the funding ended. The local foundation was too concerned about looking good—or not looking bad. Ultimately there was no community ownership or buy-in.[11] In the process of "saving the project" they had pushed everyone away from any sense of ownership of or responsibility for the project.

HP heard about the news, was concerned, and wanted to do something about it. Headquartered in Palo Alto, HP had a direct vested interest in East Palo Alto, which is in their backyard and where they had made investments in the community in the past. HP knew what kind of expertise was needed. They knew me because I was director of the MA Policy Analysis and Evaluation program at Stanford and had sent many of my students to them for evaluation internships and practicums over the years. In addition, I was on the faculty advisory board of Stanford's Haas Center for Community Service.[12] The center is responsible for training and sending students into the community to learn and to serve at the same time.[13] Many of my students were placed in the community to conduct evaluations by using the Haas Center's network. Thus the Haas Center became the natural nexus for a meeting of the minds to do something about this situation and address HP's larger concern: evaluating the Digital Village.

HP contacted the director of the Haas Center, Nadine Cruz at the time, to arrange a meeting with me. We met and they said they had heard about what we were doing in East Palo Alto and agreed with our approach (even though the local foundation was less than enthusiastic about our emphasis on local control and taking the time to build capacity and ownership). HP understood and publically said that "building capacity and sustainability takes time."

On a personal note, HP also said they thought I might be skeptical about their motives. I said I did want to know a little more about why they were investing so heavily in this project. They boldly and candidly said, "to make money." Coming from a major corporation in America, that was an unexpectedly honest answer. They had peaked my interest and of course I wanted to know more. They explained that while they were interested in making money and in contributing to the development of small businesses and related social services in the community, they were not about to sell the community equipment and software they did not need. They hoped, however, that over time people would remember who invested in them. They also hoped that their branding, including logos on their computers, printers, and digital equipment, would stick and influence small businesses to buy from Hewlett-Packard in the future. Helping to grow small businesses meant more money for HP—a burgeoning market. Their directness and clarity were a bit jarring. In retrospect, it was apparent that HP had learned that honesty was the most effective way to sell their proposition and to convince potential and skeptical business partners to join them in their enterprises. Honesty was the best policy and it worked.

This all seemed fair enough to me. The only differences in this arrangement were that there would be three sites, instead of one; a lot more money, equipment, and resources; and more time. This was an offer I could not refuse. I appreciated their candor, and I signed on to the team as the lead empowerment evaluator.

Already you can see this is not the typical, sanitized story. It is not business as usual. Instead of supporting this type of collaborative and sustained effort, the more liberal, progressive foundation had invested in the short run. The corporation, Hewlett-Packard, understood the concept of making a long-term investment, building capacity, and sustainability.

CONVERGING SELF-INTERESTS

This story is, in part, about vested interests and how they can and must overlap and converge in order to build a productive team and to produce demonstrable outcomes.

Hewlett-Packard's self-interest was on the table: to make money and to do good in the process. They wanted to help stimulate small business growth in order to improve the community and to create a new marketplace for themselves. They also wanted to be respected as a philanthropic entity and thus needed a credible assessment of their efforts.

Stanford had the expertise, pedigree for external credibility, and knowledge of the community for internal credibility. Stanford's agreement to conduct or to facilitate the evaluation solved HP's problem concerning a credible and competent evaluation. In addition, Stanford's commitment to the community was widely acknowledged and certainly uncontested. They operated one of the premier community service centers in the country. Their mission included educating students through service to the community. This agreement represented an excellent means to involve faculty and students in a large-scale, multi-cultural, complex, national project. The opportunity to learn while serving these communities was immense, attractive, and compelling.

Stanford's vested interests were to provide appropriate and meaningful ways for students to learn from real-world experience and to maintain their relationship with an old corporate friend and donor.

In addition to my role as a representative of Stanford, I had a vested interest that should be put on the table. I am the originator and founder of empowerment evaluation. Empowerment evaluation had already been used by the Accelerated Schools Project (a national educational reform movement), Stanford University Hospital, the W.K. Kellogg Foundation, an HIV prevention program, battered women's shelters, higher education (to help pass a high-stakes accreditation site visit), townships in South Africa, and Native American tribes (Fetterman, 2001; Fetterman, Kaftarian, and Wandersman, 1996; Fetterman and Wandersman, 2005).

Empowerment evaluation already had a strong track record for effectiveness, literally around the world. In addition, the principles guiding empowerment evaluation were consistent with the overall philosophical orientation guiding the project, including focusing on improvement, capacity building, and accountability. However, empowerment evaluation was still a new approach in the field. I was still looking for fertile ground to test new assumptions and techniques and to document another large-scale case example. The Digital Village allowed me to demonstrate the effectiveness of the evaluation approach. This project was an opportunity to bring the concept to scale.

At least one of the three communities knew and trusted Stanford and HP. They knew Stanford by reputation and through their community-based services. They knew me based on my own work in the community. I was also very familiar with the community because I lived there as a Stanford graduate student.

Community members also knew Hewlett-Packard as a corporate philanthropist. They were aware of Hewlett-Packard's commitment to community capacity-building projects. Community members had a short- and long-term set of vested interests. In the short run, the project was a useful revenue stream for many individuals, community-based nonprofits, and small businesses. There was also some prestige and ego associated with having a connection to HP and Stanford. East Palo Alto community members had enough experience to also look at the long term. Viewing the project from a larger perspective, the Digital Village represented an opportunity to build community capacity and to contribute to the prosperity of the community. It did not hurt that these objectives could be accomplished with two respected institutional giants in the same room.

It was a good match for everyone. It should be noted, however, although serendipity played a role, this was no accident or set of coincidences. There was a historical context and a fundamental philosophical match that made this all happen. It was a confluence of forces, specifically:

- The HP Way—with its open door policy that encourages anyone in the company to make a contribution
- HP's history of philanthropy
- Stanford's commitment to service learning through the Haas Center for Public Service
- The communities' trust and their self-help commitment to building capacity
- Empowerment evaluation's principles that align with the overall project philosophy, by focusing on improvement, community ownership, inclusion, democratic participation, social justice, community knowledge, evidence-based strategies, capacity building, organizational learning, and accountability[14]

AN EVOLVING RELATIONSHIP

The team, or ensemble, evolved over time. It seemed disjointed and disconnected in the beginning, even with the best of intentions. Phone calls were missed; emails bounced or did not include everyone that should have been on the distribution list. Missteps, mixed signals, and mistakes were made on a daily basis. Anyone who has tracked the evolution of one of their favorite sitcoms knows that the pilots and early shows are often stilted and lacking character development. Over time, the relationships grow, the individual actors' performances become more nuanced and refined, and the ensemble comes together as the actors learn how to capitalize on, play off, and enhance one another's talents. The quality of the entire series grows over time. In much the same way, this powerful combination of organizational actors matured and learned to work well together and to produce comprehensive community outcomes.

We learned that the relationship is actually closer to a marriage than a partnership. We had to get to know each other much better, including the nuances, personalities, and the small things that comprise daily life. It all started with the simple things: we all had to learn whom to call. There was always someone in each Digital Village who was the taskmaster and who prided himself or herself on punctuality, follow-through, and protocol. These individuals were the organizers and primary facilitators who brought the group together.

Once these key contacts were established (often part of the informal hierarchy, rather than the official one), interactions and transactions became smooth and reliable. In addition, we all had to learn whom to rely on (and whom to avoid) in the organization to get things done. In most cases, it was really a matter of learning what one another's strengths and weaknesses were so we knew what to expect from each other.

Once more realistic expectations were established concerning each person's abilities, responsibilities, and temperament, everyone functioned more effectively. We learned who the "smooth talker" was in both the political and the local community arenas. We also learned who the "numbers" person was in each Digital Village, since they were the ones who knew all about the figures and finances. In essence, we learned how to work with one another's strengths and weaknesses in order to get things done. In some Digital Villages we operated like a well-oiled machine. In others, we were functional but could have used a lot of WD-40 to lubricate the gears and to make the organizational wheels move a lot smoother. It took time and effort to continually work on the relationships and to learn how to function more effectively and efficiently. It also required good intent—with an eye toward the larger good for the entire family.

CONCLUSION: A PHILANTHROPIC MODEL

Hewlett-Packard's corporate philanthropy modeled this constructive, collaborative relationship, which was critical to the success of the Digital Villages.

Bess Stephens, former vice president of HP Philanthropy and Education, not only understood the power of academic prowess, or expertise, and local community ownership, she appreciated and recognized that this type of relationship takes time to cultivate and mature. According to Stephens (2003, p. 2),

> HP Philanthropy and Education has undergone a profound shift in how we align our philanthropic investments with the expertise and resources of community partners to improve people's lives. We have focused much of our energy on developing, supporting and sustaining long-term partnerships with communities, organizations and governmental agencies around the world to address substantive needs. We believe we can be most effective by teaming up with others who share our goals and our optimism.

This brief portrait of the sponsor and crew and how this team came together sets the stage for a more detailed view of the ultimate drivers of this initiative: the three Digital Villages.

3 THE DRIVERS:

THE THREE DIGITAL VILLAGES

You can't really win a race without a driver; you need someone to
drive the car.
—Kevin McCabe

Former HP Chairman and Chief Executive Officer Carly Fiorina,[1] former
President Bill Clinton,[2] and human rights activist Reverend Jesse L. Jackson
Sr.[3] helped launch the $15 million HP Digital Village project in April 2000.
This event was an important opportunity for Clinton to announce a series of
federal initiatives to bridge the digital divide and to help strengthen business
collaboratives such as HP's Digital Village. The original vision for these initiatives was to "create an informed, connected and empowered community
by combining technology, brainpower, and collaborative energy."[4] The inauguration ceremonies were held in East Palo Alto, one of the three Digital Village community sites in the United States.[5]

Although the inauguration was an all-star-studded affair, the stars of the
show, at least in this story, were the three Digital Villages. The sites competed
for these awards. Successfully bidding and winning these grants represented
an achievement in itself and required a degree of proficiency in grant writing,
marketing, and social networking. It also meant they were sufficiently net
savvy to meet the minimum technological requirements needed to launch a
digital project of this magnitude. The grant-winning community sites included
the Tribal Digital Village (San Diego area), Baltimore Digital Village (East
Baltimore), and East Palo Alto Digital Village.

The Tribal Digital Village comprised eighteen Native American reservations. The Baltimore Digital Village involved a collaboration of African American community-based organizations, ranging from Blacks in Wax (an African
American featured wax museum) to the Baltimore City Public School System.
The East Palo Alto Digital Village residents were primarily African American,

Latino, and Pacific Islanders. Projects in the East Palo Alto Digital Village ranged from Plugged In, a high-tech community resource center, to Opportunities Industrialization Center West, an employment training program that was part of the national organization founded by the former Reverend Leon Sullivan.[6] Each site was awarded $5 million, which included cash, equipment, and services over a three-year period.

HP selected these sites at least in part because of their pressing social and economic needs. However, HP also purposely selected a diverse set of communities in order to learn what might be possible among different communities facing similar challenges. Although each Digital Village created its own individual mission, the overarching mission for the projects was simple: to leapfrog[7] across the digital divide.[8] These communities were left behind in the digital age, which systematically disenfranchised them from information and opportunities.

The mission of the Digital Village project was to "provide people access to greater social and economic opportunity by closing the gap between technology-empowered and technology-excluded communities—focusing on sustainability for the communities and HP."[9] HP's role was to provide each of the Digital Villages with the necessary funds, equipment, and consultants to pursue their strategies and to accomplish their objectives.

A brief description of the three Digital Villages is provided in the following sections in order to ground this abstract comprehensive social change initiative in concrete community settings. A more detailed examination of the empowerment evaluation engine used to help drive this social intervention will follow in the next chapter.

TRIBAL DIGITAL VILLAGE

The history of Native American mistreatment is well documented in American history textbooks, from the concept of manifest destiny[10] to the cries of Wounded Knee,[11] as well as the controversy surrounding Alcatraz Island.[12] Native American reservations are typically isolated, impoverished communities that are plagued with high unemployment and drug and alcohol problems.[13]

The Tribal Digital Village was a network of eighteen Native American reservations and over 7,600 Native Americans in the San Diego area. Most of the reservations were struggling financially. However, a few were prosperous, primarily as a result of gaming activities. The Tribal Digital Village was awarded a $5 million grant from HP in 2001, as part of the larger $15 million HP Digital Village project. The Tribal Digital Village focused on economic development, education, and culture. Technology was used to build on existing kinship networks and cultural traditions.[14]

Signature Projects

The most significant achievement, or signature project, was the creation of "the largest unlicensed wireless systems in the United States," according to the head of the U.S. Federal Communications Commission (FCC). The FCC continues to recognize the Tribal Digital Village's accomplishments in this area. The Tribal Digital Village is characterized in FCC documents as "one of the shining examples in wireless unregulated spectrums that's connected several tribes here" (U.S. Federal Communications Commission 2009, p. 70). It became the digital backbone of the tribes' communication system. It was linked with a project supported by the National Science Foundation, the High-Performance Wireless Research and Education Network,[15] which connects the tribal offices, community centers, schools, and individual residences of the eighteen reservations.

This point is significant because communication across the reservations was fragmented at best before this system was created and almost nonexistent outside the boundaries of the reservations. This was in large part due to the efforts of an earlier incarnation of the Bureau of Indian Affairs from 1900 to 1970.[16] Building a reliable communication system within and outside the reservation had tremendous symbolic and real-world significance for the tribes (see Figure 1).

The communication system was also used to support museum activities, contributing to the preservation of important cultural artifacts. Their Internet portal (SCTDV.net) also served as a community information source, discussion board, and accessible calendar of community events (see Figure 2).

The second signature project was the Tribal Print Source, formerly the Hi Rez printing service. It provided digital imaging and printing services.

FIGURE 1. Tribal Digital Village videoconferencing outside the reservation with Dr. Fetterman and his class at Stanford University.

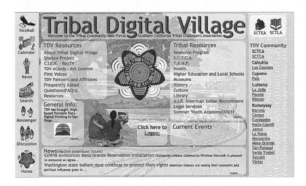

FIGURE 2. Tribal Digital Village's Internet portal. *Source*: TDV Internet Portal.

HP donated the digital press, service, and technical support. The press was a large-scale version of its smaller technology grant or donation program. It was designed to jump-start small entrepreneurial businesses in the community. In this case, the press not only generated a profit, it helped to support other programs on the reservations. The creation of the press is notable because it is a form of economic sustainability that both HP and the tribes had envisioned.

The press also represents an alternative for Native Americans living on the reservation. According to Denis Turner, executive director of the Southern California Tribal Chairmen's Association (SCTCA), which housed the Tribal Digital Village, "We're searching for alternatives to gaming as a vehicle for financial independence. HP's involvement with the Tribal Digital Village has given us an opportunity to own, develop and operate high-technology businesses."

EAST PALO ALTO DIGITAL VILLAGE

Launched in April 2000, the East Palo Alto Digital Village was the first HP Digital Village. Its location was a low-income, minority community characterized by high crime and drug use. At one point it was labeled the "murder capital" of the nation.[17] However, thanks to a drug enforcement agency task force and to community resolve and cooperation, crime has been significantly reduced. At the time of the Digital Village initiative, the community was transitioning from an African American majority into a Latino majority and African American minority population. There is also a visible and active Pacific Islander presence in the community. This ethnic transition has added new life to the community but with some accompanying tensions as people adjust to shifts in political power in the city.

East Palo Alto is across the highway from Palo Alto, an affluent, primarily white community. The economic contrast of large, multi-million dollar homes in Palo Alto on the west side of the freeway and small, and in many cases, deteriorating homes on the east side was and continues to be striking. However, East Palo Alto's proximity to Stanford University, only a few miles away, has made it the recipient of an ongoing stream of student and faculty talent and funds to address serious social and economic problems in the community.

East Palo Alto was awarded the same $5 million to operate as the other Digital Villages. The community partnership comprised schools, businesses, government, and local service organizations. The focus of the initiative was on community self-empowerment and economic self-sufficiency.

Signature Projects

The East Palo Alto Digital Village had a host of signature projects that spoke to their accomplishments. They included the Community Network, Belle Haven E:learning Project, Small Business Development Initiative, and the Community Academy.

The Community Network consisted of three organizational initiatives: EPA.net, Technology Access Points, and Community Grants Program. EPA.net was an online resource center that provided a shared space for public announcements and a forum for community discussions designed to solve community problems (see Figure 3). Technology Access Points (TAP) were local community sites where residents learned to use computers and access the Internet to improve their daily lives. The Community Grants Program provided technological tools for small nonprofit organizations. It enabled them to provide a higher level of service to residents.

The Belle Haven E:learning Project provided laptops to 400 students in grades 4–8 at Belle Haven School. Teachers also received laptops. The project transformed the learning environment.[18] The Internet became a core curricular resource for the school and transformed teaching and learning in the school.

The Small Business Development Initiative delivered technology equipment and training to small business owners. The initiative contributed to the community's economic development by building small business technological capacity.

The Community Academy was an employment and skills training center that provided services to the signature projects, local nonprofits, and local residents. It helped to build program capacity by teaching people specific employable skills. Sharon Williams, the executive director of the academy had high hopes for this initiative. She said, "I see a new door opening up for all of us in East Palo Alto. It is like a new day, like Rev. Leon Sullivan used to say: 'It's a chance to get our fair share, our piece of the economic pie.'"[19]

FIGURE 3. East Palo Alto Digital Village's Internet portal. *Source*: East Palo Alto Digital Village Internet portal.

BALTIMORE DIGITAL VILLAGE

The Baltimore Digital Village began in 2001, a year after the East Palo Alto site. It was located in East Baltimore, a primarily African American community with a growing Latino population. East Baltimore's socioeconomics were troubling at the time with 40 percent living below the poverty line. Crime, drug abuse, and physical safety and security issues were so pervasive in the community that they were largely taken for granted, just part of the background of everyday life in the community.[20]

Counterbalancing these community conditions, the Baltimore Digital Village was situated in the heart of the one of President Bill Clinton's Empowerment Zones.[21] Empowerment Zones were part of his landmark legislation in 1994. The legislation provided $100 million in cash and $250 million in wage tax credits over a ten-year period to six Empowerment Zones. The seed money was used to revitalize underserved areas with the aim of forging public-private partnerships dedicated to increasing the quality of life in those communities.

Another advantage of the Baltimore Digital Village, and in part the basis for their selection, was access to existing local community-based organizations as well as to local businesses and to the school system. It was therefore ironic that although BDV efforts were primarily focused on building the capacity of local organizations and businesses, recommending business strategies such as incorporation or formal nonprofit 501(c)3 status, the Baltimore

Digital Village did not adopt its own advice. It was the only village managed by a committee or a temporary coalition. This was symbolic and a red flag. It foreshadowed future events as many of their efforts stalled or never made it out the door. Their story is in part one of organizational instability. Nevertheless, they were recognized for their efforts to create a digital community designed to facilitate youth and adult learning services.

Signature Projects

The Baltimore Digital Village had three signature projects. They included BDV@Community, BDV@School, and BDV@Work. Each of these projects had multiple supporting initiatives and activities.

The BDV@Community enhanced community access to computers and to the Internet. It provided 300 families with their own computer and printer. Computer skills training courses were provided in order to help families maximize the benefits of their computer equipment. One family used the equipment and training to grow their home daycare business. The initiative also included the creation of six "hubs," or technology centers, throughout the community to provide residents with continued computer training, access to the Internet, and employment training opportunities. The community portal was only accessible to East Baltimore citizens associated with BDV; however, it provided them with email access and online storage capacity. It was designed to be the digital information source that focused on the concerns of the community, including information about jobs, educational opportunities, and health care.

The cornerstone of the BDV@School was its partnership with the Baltimore City Public School System.[22] They adopted five schools and integrated computer equipment and training into the school curriculum. The computer equipment included peripherals such as digital cameras, printers, and scanners as well as software. The training effort was focused on 185 teachers who were provided with computers and were instructed in their use, with the aim of enhancing their teaching and infusing the technology into the classroom. According to Carmen V. Russo, chief executive officer of the Baltimore City Public School System, "The technology and support that the Baltimore Digital Village has provided our teachers and students has proved invaluable in our efforts to develop an outstanding curriculum."[23]

BDV@Work was a collaboration between employers and employment training centers. It provided professional development training programs to better prepare East Baltimore citizens for local business needs and requirements by helping thirty graduates secure employment. The Small Business Development Initiative provided thirty-five local business owners with technology packages, a five-week skills training program, and business services consultations. Employers and training programs were accessible through the Web (BDV portal) and the community help desk. This made accessing the portal more meaningful, relevant, and necessary. BDV@Work also fostered the development of fifty small businesses in the community by providing them with both equipment and training.

BDV worked closely with a variety of community centers such as Blacks in Wax (Figure 4), Education Based Latino Outreach (EBLO), and *Kids Scoop* (youth newspaper) to provide computer-training service centers to enhance computer literacy in the community.

Former mayor Martin O'Malley was so impressed with the Digital Village's contributions that he proclaimed June 11, 2003 to be "Baltimore Digital

The Digital Village Partnership

The Digital Village Partnership is a $5 million initiative of Hewlett Packard (HP). The Museum is one of six Community Technology Centers of the Baltimore Digital Village. A computer lab has been installed in the Museum's administrative office building, located at 1649 East North Avenue. The computer lab offers public access to digital village residents during and after museum hours and to East Baltimore HP schools during regular museum hours of operation.

FIGURE 4. Blacks in Wax's "hub" connection to the Baltimore Digital Village. *Source*: Great Blacks in Wax Museum, Baltimore, Maryland.

Village Day." A year later (June 29, 2004), he continued to express his support and praise for the program.

> HP is playing an vital and much needed role in providing the people of Baltimore with expanded and sustainable access to technology. . . . The East Baltimore Digital Village is a landmark public-private partnership and, together, we are changing lives through the use of technology.[24]

CONCLUSION

By providing these brief descriptions of the Digital Villages' activities, I hope to have put a face to their names. These are just a few of the success stories celebrated by the Digital Villages. These are solid outcomes with tremendous face-validity, designed to generate sustainable economic and social development in the community long after this influx of seed money and support is gone. It may appear unusual to begin with the end of the story, but it helps to signal why this experience is important to unpack. In this case, it is the ride or the journey itself that is as important as the destination.

The next chapter describes the empowerment evaluation engine that was the driving force behind the development of local *evaluation* capacity building. It complemented these *program-based* capacity building efforts, by giving the Digital Villages a tool to monitor and evaluate their own programs. Empowerment evaluation became a powerful tool to help the Digital Villages accomplish their goals and objectives—their dreams and aspirations.

4 THE ENGINE:

EMPOWERMENT EVALUATION

> If everything seems under control, you're just not
> going fast enough.
> —Mario Andretti

A mission as ambitious and as grassroots in orientation as that of the Digital Village project required an evaluation approach philosophically and methodologically aligned with the challenge. Empowerment evaluation was selected to help the three communities plan, implement, assess, and improve their work. This approach differs from many other forms of evaluation or strategic planning because the groups or communities remain in control of the process. In addition, although it is best to begin an empowerment evaluation at the planning stage of a program, it can be used at any stage of program development, including the beginning of implementation, the middle, and the end of a program funding cycle. The evaluation simply focuses on continued operations and sustainability concerning the eminent demise of a funding stream.

One of the most important features of empowerment evaluation for Digital Village community members was that it could operate in high gear almost immediately. The opportunity to build the Digital Village was a race against time. The project timelines were tight, but more important, many community members thought they had lost or wasted too many years working with community programs and projects that never got past the starting line, when vital work was needed in their communities. It was time to get their lives back on track, with an empowerment evaluation road map and a crew to assist them, so that they could begin to move at breakneck speed and make up for lost time.

BACKGROUND AND DEFINITION

Empowerment evaluation (Fetterman, 1994, 2001; Fetterman, Kaftarian, and Wandersman, 2006; Fetterman and Wandersman, 2005, 2007) has been used by the National Aeronautics and Space Administration's Jet Propulsion Laboratory to educate youth about the prototype Mars Rover,[1] townships in South Africa to create sustainable community health initiatives, the U.S. Department of Education's Office of Special Education and Rehabilitation Services to foster self-determination, the Centers for Disease Control and Prevention to prevent and reduce intimate partner violence and sexual violence,[2] and with Native American tribes to build technological and economic infrastructures on reservations.[3] In addition, it has been used in a wide variety of areas, including schools in academic distress (Fetterman, 2005), accreditation in higher education (Fetterman, 2001, 2012b), minority tobacco prevention (Fetterman, 2005), and medical education (Fetterman, 2009; Fetterman, Deitz, and Gesundheit, 2010).

Empowerment evaluation is the use of evaluation concepts and techniques to foster self-determination[4] and program improvement (Fetterman, 1994, 2001). An expanded definition helps to explain what the approach is designed to accomplish:

> Empowerment evaluation is an evaluation approach that aims to increase the probability of achieving program success by (1) providing program stakeholders with tools for assessing the planning, implementation, and self-evaluation of their program, and (2) mainstreaming evaluation as part of the planning and management of the program/organization.[5]

In essence, empowerment evaluation is not a neutral, "objective" scientific experiment that succeeds or fails based on the data and leaves the community with nothing if the findings are not statistically significant. The needs of the community remain. That idealized view may be appealing to some, but it is a false conception of what science[6] and evaluation are all about (Berk and Rossi, 1976; Conrad, 1994; Fetterman, 1982; Greene, 1997; House, 1998; Novick, 1998).

Empowerment evaluation is honest and rigorous, but it is designed to help people accomplish their objectives. There are no guarantees, but like a financial advisor, empowerment evaluation improves the probabilities of success. It is as concerned about contribution as it is about attribution. In addition, empowerment evaluation is not a short-term process of episodic observation and judgment; on the contrary, it becomes a part of the fabric of an organization. According to Scriven (1997a, p. 174),

> Devolving some of the responsibility for evaluation is good. A program whose staff are not doing reasonably good evaluation of their own program is incompetently staffed, at some or all levels. Empowerment evaluation is doing something important to reduce that deficit.

Empowerment evaluation fosters lifelong learning on both an individual and organizational level. Empowerment evaluation is designed to build capacity for the long haul and to contribute to meaningful community sustainability.

Empowerment Theory

Three theories guide empowerment evaluation: process use, theories of action, and theories of use (Argyris and Schön, 1978; Fetterman, 2004; Patton, 1997b). Together they represent a highly combustible social fuel that powers the empowerment evaluation engine.

Process use proposes that the more people participate in evaluating their own program, the more likely they are to buy into the findings and the recommendations—because they are their findings and recommendations. They begin to think like evaluators. It is often the case that community members and program staff have to stand on the sidelines while their program is being evaluated and their future is being determined by others—typically outsiders. This is a serious problem, as Scriven (1997a, p. 12) highlights,

> One should not have to add that external evaluators will sometimes miss deep problems that are obvious to Staff and that often have less credibility with Staff than the empowerment evaluator, and often for that or other reasons, there is less chance that their recommendations will be implemented.

Empowerment evaluation places them back in the driver's seat where they belong. Credibility on this personal level creates trust, which is the social oil than enables the gears of an evaluation to turn. Without it, the brakes screech and everything freezes in its tracks. In essence, trust leads to participation, participation leads to ownership, and ownership leads to use. It all contributes to the greater social good.

The theory of action is the espoused theory or what the organization professes to be about. Most organizations make lofty statements about their values and ideals. They are the dreams and aspirations of a group, organization, or community.

The theory of use is the actual observed behavior of individuals or organizations. It is what people do in real life. Theories of action rarely match theories of use. Empowerment evaluation is designed to provide a continual feedback loop with the aim of reconciling theories of action with those of use. In other words, empowerment evaluation helps people walk their talk, that is, to align their aspirational statements with their actual day-to-day behavior.[7]

Empowerment Concepts

Empowerment evaluation concepts help guide this respectful and effective approach. They are like lenses in which to see the world and to ensure that we appropriately conceptualize the task ahead. These concepts range from a culture of evidence to reflective practitioners. Together they form a synergistic force that catapults the person, project, or program forward into a meaningful momentum with a focused sense of purpose.

A Culture of Evidence. First, empowerment evaluation helps develop a culture of evidence[8] to ensure that data are used to inform decision making, instead of relying on personal and political beliefs. This is important because most Digital Village community members were not trained to use evidence in this way. However, using evidence instead of personal or political persuasion appealed to them because it was logical (seemed like common sense), transparent (the information was not hidden from view), and fair (anyone could question the information). In addition, it was more open than the politics of power that had operated in projects in their communities in the past.

A Critical Friend. Second, empowerment evaluation relies on the use of a critical friend[9] to facilitate the effort. Such friends are supportive, but also critical and honest. They believe in the project or initiative, but it is precisely because they have a vested interest in seeing the project work that they are critical. They also help to keep the effort rigorous and on target. Their role in the project contrasts sharply with the more conventional external evaluators who may have little if any connection with the community or commitment to the outcomes of the project. Such evaluators see themselves as independent and objective. Some go so far as to view themselves as uncontaminated by local contact and personal feelings. This belief is based on the false premise or assumption that independent, completely objective observers exist, or that any assessment is neutral and uninfluenced by the political or socioeconomic context.[10] The "distant, objective, removed" position is neither feasible nor desirable. Evaluators who define their role this narrowly typically commit only a fraction of the time displayed by evaluators who are invested and committed to the success of the endeavor.

Cycles of Reflection and Action. Third, cycles of reflection and action are characteristic of empowerment evaluations. In traditional forms of evaluation, data are collected but rarely used to inform decision making. Reports typically gather dust. In contrast, empowerment evaluation data are routinely collected, considered, discussed, and used to inform action steps. Once a decision is made based on the data and new strategies are implemented, the new intervention is also evaluated—thus the cycle of reflection and action.[11]

A Community of Learners. Fourth, empowerment evaluations help to cultivate a community of learners.[12] Community and program staff members, as well as program participants, learn from each other as they go or as they implement the program. The group creates a "safe environment" to brainstorm and to contribute to the task, to address the problems, and to improve practice. Through critique and dialogue, tackling difficult problems and generating new strategies to improve program performance become normal healthy group functions.

The Digital Village's community of learners were also a project-based, real-world, experiential training ground. It provided people with a chance to simultaneously build a program and a learning organization[13] together. Few Digital Village staff and community members were given this kind of opportunity in the past. The Digital Village experience gave them a group voice to shape their community's future. This was a profound opportunity. It foreshadows the issue of capacity building, discussed at greater length in Chapter 9.

Reflective Practitioners. Fifth, this type of engagement helps to develop reflective practitioners.[14] These are individuals who learn how to continually reflect on their own practice and to improve it. This development is one of the most important sustainable contributions made by empowerment evaluation because this mindset can be applied and taught to others over a lifetime—building long-term transferable capacity in the community.

Empowerment Steps

Empowerment evaluation can be applied in a variety of ways, ranging from a three-step to a ten-step approach.[15] It can rely on the use of basic tools, such as poster paper, magic markers, and spreadsheets, or more elaborate technologies including graphic artists, LCD (liquid crystal display) projectors, collaborative webpages, and shared online documents, as well as videoconferencing over the net.[16] The logic of the approach, however, is what counts.

The Digital Villages employed a three-step approach, which included (1) establishing a mission (2) taking stock, and (3) planning for the future. The group began the process by crafting its mission, or vision. The mission step was facilitated by an empowerment evaluator or critical friend. Notes of the group's views were recorded on poster paper (and on a laptop computer, with the contents of the computer screen projected on a wall with an LCD projector). The mission represented the values of the group as a collaborative. This step was important because it represented the foundation of the evaluation. A couple of Digital Village administrators wanted to dispense with this step because they already had a mission statement, but a fundamental question was raised: Who wrote it? Was it the grant writer, the director, or even a small group of staff members who have long since moved on to other agencies? It was important to take the time to find out what the present group thought and valued because they represented the driving force in the community. It was that intellectual and emotional energy that was tapped for the long journey ahead.

At the same time, mission statements are not created in a vacuum. Pre-existing mission statements are respected, valued, and considered. In some cases pre-existing mission statements continue in force and sub-missions are created. One of the things that makes this process meaningful and effective is that it aligns precisely with what the organization or community is being held accountable for already. Within this context, people can determine (with the assistance of an empowerment evaluator) precisely what they can do to accomplish their objectives, to reach their goals, and to produce their desired outcomes. This process simply asks what can you do within this context to make the mission a reality. (In the process of single loop[17] learning in an empowerment evaluation, in which group members focus on ways to implement, repair, and improve existing polices and practices, double loop[18] learning emerges. In double loop learning, members of the group come up with new ideas that rock the foundations of the institution's way of thinking and doing business.)

After crafting a mission, the group took stock of, or assessed, where they were in their efforts. (This step can be applied to the planning phase as well if an organization has not launched or is not fully functional or operational.) Taking stock has two stages: setting priorities and rating, or assessing. The critical friend asked members of the group to generate a list of critical program activities. It was a brainstorming session, in which suggestions were not censored, voted on, or assessed. The list represented the group's view of the most important things to focus on and evaluate as a group at that time. Once the list was completed, each individual was given five sticky dots. They placed the dots on the activities they thought were the most important to evaluate as a group from that point on throughout the initiative. Once the dots were placed on the activities list, the dots were counted. The activities with the most dots were selected for the rating step of the process. It was also informative to reflect on the activities that did not receive many dots. It did not mean that those activities were not important. However, they were not the most important to the group at that stage in the development of the initiative or the organization's growth. In some cases, the group thought they were doing sufficiently well in that area or that the supervisor or some other party was managing that activity adequately and that their energy could be better spent on the remaining activities.

Once the list was complete, the group was asked to rate each activity on a 1 (low) to 10 (high) point scale. It was important to remind everyone that this rating was not a ranking—theoretically every activity could have been rated a three or a seven. It was also important to remind everyone which rating was high (10) and low (1) because people often get the rating code confused. One of the features of this approach is that errors are expected and can be corrected rapidly, with no loss of face or time. This is particularly true since the ratings were recorded in an Excel spreadsheet with formulas already entered. A change in the rating resulted in a corresponding change in the total and bar chart.

The facilitator or critical friend asked members of the group to provide their reasons (and evidence) for their ratings. A low rating for communication, for example, elicited the following explanations from Digital Village members: "We don't talk to each other"; "There is never an agenda for any of our meetings"; "There is no opportunity to simply sit and chat about what we are doing anymore"; and "I feel we are talking past each other." The reasons for the low ratings provide not only evidence for the rating but a direction to build on in the "planning for the future" step of the empowerment evaluation process. The absence of an agenda for weekly meetings, for example, was easily remedied. Providing an agenda immediately improved one level of organizational communication.

The heart of "taking stock" is this honest and engaged dialogue[19] about the reasons for the communities' successes and failures. The numbers, at this point, are really a jumping-off point for in-depth discussion and debate. Taking stock provided people with a rare opportunity to examine and to improve something neglected and broken in their world. It also provided them with a window of opportunity to build on strengths and to improve things they were already doing well.

Taking stock was a time for the elephant in the room to appear (Zerubavel, 2006).[20] In one case, there was uneven staffing, producing organizational tensions and jealousies. In another case, people were being underpaid. The topics that no one wanted to discuss, but which were slowly eroding the confidence and energy of the group, were raised and addressed. Taking stock is also the most common space for the "aha" moments, in which important organizational insights surface. They are moments of clarity about what's working or not working on a fundamental and systemic level. They may be an epiphany about who is in charge of the program or an imbalance in the workload in which one group has more staff than another but a lighter workload.

They are really the accumulation of connected ideas that appears as an instantaneous epiphany in what Johnson (2010) refers to as the "liquid network," or in this case the "taking stock" exercise. One of the Digital Villages, for example, came to the stark realization (in the middle of a "taking stock" exchange) that they were not going to be a sustainable enterprise unless they assumed a more confident attitude, seized the authority entrusted to them, and initiated plans to incorporate. This knowledge enabled them to take steps toward becoming a fiscally responsible entity with a life of its own.

In a "conventional" evaluation, completing the "taking stock" step would have been sufficient, even an ending point. It is in essence, a rating, an assessment, and even including dialogue, a review or critique of the assessment. However, in an empowerment evaluation, this is only the beginning. It is a launching point for new interventions, goals, and strategies. The Digital Villages created a plan for the future, after engaging in this internal dialogue about the status of the group's activities. The plans for the future were a form of strategic planning, with specific goals, strategies, and credible forms of evidence. They did not pick just any goals. The goals had to be linked to the activities they had just evaluated and discussed. The planning for the future goals were purposely simple. For example, one of the Digital Village activities was communication, thus the goal became "to improve communication." They were the ones who selected the strategies, not an outsider or "external expert." Many of the strategies were directly linked to the evidence they produced when justifying their ratings during the "taking stock" step. The evidence was credible to the funder, the community, and the evaluation coach or critical friend. It became a moment of shared understanding, responsibility, and commitment. It also ensured that no one, including the funder, could pull the rug out from under the group at the last minute by changing the rules (of evidence) in the middle or end of the game and thus trivialize their efforts and demoralize the group.

This process was cyclical. Traditional evaluation methods, such as interviews, surveys, and observations were used to test whether their strategies were working. This enabled members of the community to make corrections as needed, based on this continual evaluative feedback loop.[21] The group conducted additional formal assessments of their activities and compared their assessments with their previous ratings of key activities. This enabled them to measure change over time and to determine if they were making progress and approximating their goals. In other words, the initial taking stock exercise represented the groups' baseline for future comparison. The plans for the future represented the program intervention. A second taking stock exercise represented a second data point, enabling the group to measure growth or change over time by comparing the baseline ratings with the second data point ratings.

Many other conventional evaluation tools were used in this Digital Village empowerment evaluation, particularly during the planning for the future step of the process. For example, we (1) established a baseline, (2) agreed on a goal, (3) created benchmarks, and (4) compared actual performance with planned benchmarks. The common denominator in empowerment evaluation is the creation of a continual feedback loop on performance.[22] This is where triple-loop[23]learning takes place, the continual challenging and assessing of fundamental values, beliefs, and norms with an eye toward strategically catapulting the organization into a socioeconomically competitive marketplace of ideas and services in the future. Such learning is also the source of innovation in a healthy learning organization. (For details and free guides, see the empowerment webpage and blog at http://www.davidfetterman.com/empowerment evaluation.htm and http://eevaluation.blogspot.com.)

CONCLUSION

Empowerment evaluation was used throughout the entire project. It helped people make decisions informed by the data. It helped them build their capacity to evaluate their own performance. The process also ensured a measure of intellectual coherence since the community's plans for the future were rooted in their ratings, or evaluation, of the program. Their evaluation of the program was rooted in their mission, which represented the community's deeply held and shared values.

Intellectual coherence is critical to empowerment evaluation's success as a tool for systemic, comprehensive community change. Each step planted the seeds for the next step. For example, the reasons and evidence provided by a member of the community to justify a high or a low rating during the taking stock step was the same evidence needed to determine if their new plans for the future were working and progress was being made.

The entire effort was also an exercise in efficiency. The group started with the mission, or big picture, which was reduced to the bare essentials during taking stock, and used the indicators and evidence in taking stock to implement new strategies and monitor performance. Instead of coming up with a handful of "brilliant" but irrelevant solutions to problems that didn't even exist (and thus dissipating the group's limited resources), empowerment evaluation helped the Digital Village communities identify real problems and propose relevant strategies to resolve those specific problems.

Empowerment evaluation also institutionalized evaluation, so that it became a part of the planning and the management of the project.[24] Empowerment evaluation became a tool to help infuse the "HP Way" into the Digital Village's grassroots effort. It became a part of the infrastructure that made this project successful. This tool helped to produce real, demonstrable outcomes and results. It serviced a wide range of clients, programs, and projects from small business start-ups to senior centers.

We are done running laps around the track and getting warmed up. In the next three chapters, the Digital Village experience is presented through the lens of the three steps of empowerment evaluation: (1) establishing a mission, (2) taking stock, and (3) planning for the future. This analysis places the Digital Village experience under a microscope and focuses on the communities' organizational development and evolution through each step of the process. These chapters also highlight the power of this approach to facilitate large-scale, community-based change initiatives. The race is about to begin.

5 THE STARTING LINE: THE MISSION

If you wait, all that happens is that you get older.
—Mario Andretti

The sponsor, the crew, and the drivers have all been introduced including Hewlett-Packard, Stanford University, three Digital Villages, and a host of individual projects. We have even looked under the hood and inspected the empowerment evaluation engine and the fuel feeding this initiative—the desire for a better life. You are probably asking at this point in the story: What are they going to do next? How are they going to make sense out of all this? Well, Digital Village participants posed the same set of questions.

- Tribal Digital Village member: What the heck are we supposed to do now?
- East Palo Alto Digital Village member: Anyone have any ideas about where we need to go next?
- Baltimore Digital Village member: Where do we even begin?

These questions may sound surprising given the detailed presentations made to Hewlett-Packard to secure the grant, the vibrancy and the effectiveness of the existing community network, and the amount of work already accomplished. These were, however, honest questions. They are not uncommon questions in large-scale community-change projects. A flag should go up if you don't hear these kinds of questions. Not hearing them is the sign of an overconfident group, who are oblivious to the road hazards ahead and not seasoned enough to know when to ask for help. These were competent, hard-working, and committed communities. However, they had never faced a challenge of this scope, or magnitude, before. They were asking precisely the right questions at precisely the right time in their journey.

Additional questions bubbled up from each Digital Village: Do we create a plan for each Digital Village and each project? Do we set up goals and objectives immediately with firm timelines? At this point, empowerment evalua-tion stepped in, as it were, and was able to respond to many of these funda-mental questions.

The questions and suggestions were all appropriate and logical. However, they were premature. It was important to take a few steps back and begin from the beginning. The appropriate questions at that point in time were the following:

- Who are we? What is important to us? What are our values?

- What are we trying to do? What are we trying to accomplish?

- What do we want to see at the end of the day? What does the future look like for all of us? How do we define prosperity and describe what it means to enhance the quality of life in our community?

These are the big questions: the mission questions. The mission sets the tone for the entire project and for the evaluation. According to Kubisch et al. (2010), "Ensuring that all actors are in agreement about the core purpose of the work is critical to creating and maintaining focus." As my dad used to say, "If you don't know where you are going, any road will get you there." He was right and that's what happens to many large-scale community initiatives. They miss a step and proceed, often at breakneck speed, down a path without any real sense of direction. This approach can be dangerous for a community, bring-ing the best of intentions to a crashing halt. Ironically, it is not the speed that is the problem. Moving fast in an initiative is not good or bad, it just happens as you get better at doing what you do. It is the lack of direction combined with speed that is a recipe for disaster. You have to have some idea where the finish line is. Many large-scale initiatives never take the time to dream out loud as part of a group or community, to give those dreams both a voice and a name, and to memorialize those dreams on paper or digitized recordings. This point is where the Digital Village story really begins.

This chapter highlights the process of developing a mission in each of the Digital Villages. A description of this step in the process, along with a brief commentary, sheds light on many of the how and why questions associated with the creation of a mission statement. The values expressed by each Digital Village differed. They took on different shapes and configurations. As such, each of their individual mission statements pointed them in a clear, authentic, and unique direction, faithfully reflecting ideals they publically espoused. The time devoted to this deceptively simple task paid off for each one of them. This exercise helped them focus their goals, proceed in a timely manner, and efficiently produce their desired outcomes.

SURFACING THE MISSION

The first step in the process of developing a mission involves selecting an empowerment evaluator to guide or to facilitate the group. The sponsor typically offers the community this resource, but the community makes the final decision on whether to make use of a critical friend. Next, it is important to invite as many relevant people to the event as possible. If key groups or constituents are not invited, the participating group may lose a dynamic and potentially powerful contribution, may alienate a partner who could then seek to undermine or to sabotage the process, and may need to duplicate the effort at a later date to incorporate the neglected group's input.

The process is simple: the empowerment evaluator solicits ideas about the mission of the organization or program from members of the community. The empowerment evaluator helps the group to focus on a higher conceptual plane, that is, on their dreams rather than on their activities. It is difficult for most groups to launch into a discussion about their mission because they are immersed in the moment, the day-to-day. They must be given enough time to brainstorm, to listen to each other, and to feel comfortable taking a risk. In addition, most groups will commingle their ideas about mission and program activities. It is the empowerment evaluator's responsibility to diplomatically help the group place their ideas in appropriate "conceptual bins." The empowerment evaluator may rhetorically ask participants if they think their idea is part of their mission, or dream of the future, or an activity to help them make that dream a reality. They will typically respect the difference and in the process educate others in the group concerning the level of abstraction desired for this step of the empowerment evaluation process. Key phrases are recorded on poster sheet paper, ideally by a community member, and posted on the walls to remind participants of what they stated throughout the exercise. A member of the group and the empowerment evaluator draft a rough mission statement based on the exchange. The group reviews, critiques, and ultimately approves it. However, this initial drafting is done in the background, not during the exercise, otherwise it would slow down the process. A brief description of the mission step in each Digital Village provides an insight into the communities' values and aspirations at the beginning of this race.

TRIBAL DIGITAL VILLAGE

It was a typical warm, sunny day in southern California. But it was no ordinary day. We had assembled a prestigious body of sovereign nations all under one roof in the hills of San Diego. Tribes and affiliates in attendance included Viejas,[1] Jamul,[2] Barona,[3] Los Coyotes,[4] Campo,[5] Santa Ysabel,[6] Manzanita,[7] San Pasqual,[8] Pala,[9] Pauma,[10] Rincon,[11] La Jolla,[12] Inaja-Cosmit,[13] Mesa Grande,[14] La Posta,[15] Sycuan,[16] Ewiiaaapaayp,[17] and the Southern California Tribal Chairmen's Association.[18] It was the first time all eighteen bodies had assembled for a project of this magnitude. The meeting was designed to initiate the Tribal Digital Village empowerment evaluation. There was excitement and anticipation and some skepticism in the air.

Professor Linda Locklear[19] (a member of one of the tribes) and I asked everyone to contribute their thoughts about the mission or purpose of the Tribal Digital Village. One elder said "economic opportunity." Another tribal member said "communication and cooperation." The list of ideas and terms began to flow, including "preservation of cultural identity," "tribal sovereignty," "job creation," "self-sufficiency," "making technology accessible," and "helping expose youth to new opportunities and preparing them for the future." We recorded the tribal mission comments on poster paper. We also had the luxury of having graphic artists[20] illustrate our thoughts on poster paper that we taped to the walls during the exercise. The generation of ideas and values continued until we reached a saturation point, and then we stopped and paused. It was one of those awkward pregnant pauses where most people felt a little uncomfortable with the empty space and the silence. However, this gave everyone enough time to think, to reflect, and to crystallize their thoughts. This empty space allowed big-picture ideas to surface. What emerged, in this case, could not have been scripted. One voice shouted out from the back of the room, "build capacity." Those words stuck. They became the glue that united the group. It was an idea they all shared. It is also one of the basic principles guiding empowerment evaluation.

It was time to bring this hour or hour and a half to a close—that's all the time we normally spend on the mission step of the process. Otherwise, people's eyes begin to glaze over. In addition, there is a law of diminishing returns that applies to this kind of exercise, as is evidenced by an increase in the repetition of posted topics. Linda and I asked one of the participants to take the lead in drafting their mission statement. It is important to pull people into every step of the process and to allow them to take control of it, from the earliest stages of the evaluation. This involvement is what creates buy-in, ownership, and commitment throughout the effort. (It is the process use theory in action, discussed earlier in Chapter 4.)

We started to draft the mission statement during the break, between the mission and taking stock step of the process. However, most of the mission statement was written off line, later in the week. We did not want to slow down the process and interfere with the group momentum as we shifted gears to take stock of the effort.

We also consulted with some of the elders during the week, concerning previous efforts to define the mission(s) of the tribes. We folded those contributions into our summary mission statement. It was important to respect the work of the elders and their previous contributions to unify the tribes. At the same time, we all agreed that it was of utmost importance to honor the group that was present at the moment. They represented the critical mass, the energy, and the force that would drive us forward, shaping the community's future. We circulated the draft among the tribal members, received feedback, revised, and then posted the final version of the mission, which is given here:

Tribal Digital Village Mission Statement

The Tribal Digital Village will create and sustain a communications and information network to assist San Diego County Indian Reservations to achieve goals in the areas of economic, educational, and community development while preserving and protecting cultural identity and tribal sovereignty. New technology is a tool that when combined with community-led programs will create economic opportunities through education, skill development, and job creation and will help local tribes in their move towards economic self-sufficiency. Tribal Digital Village networks will enhance communication and share information between tribes to help promote a sense of community, a spirit of cooperation, and respect for culture and language. The accessibility of technology to both individuals and tribal governments closes the geographical and emotional distance that exists between people and between organizations. Closing this gap will allow all tribal people, particularly the youth in our rural communities, to experience a broader reality and benefit from a new range of choices. The Tribal Digital Village will also provide us with an opportunity to build capacity particularly among our youth. It will help them prepare for the future enriching and enhancing our spirit and identity.

The final mission statement represented the group's values at that slice in time. We were not aiming at perfection. We were not purists. Other members of the group were able to refine it later for the purpose of producing brochures, proposals, and related publications. We just wanted to get the main thoughts down, to construct a democratically formed statement of our values, and to provide the group with an opportunity to eliminate any ideas that they thought did not belong in the mission statement.

The mission statement served as a foundational building block throughout the evaluation. It helped to create an intellectual coherence to the effort. As the group shifted into "taking stock" and "planning for the future" exercises, they were guided by the values represented in the mission statement. Moreover, the outcomes of the effort could be tied to the mission itself, particularly economic sustainability, enhanced communication, and building capacity among youth. The entire exercise of creating a mission statement helped to forge the earliest traces of an inter-tribally based Digital Village community.

EAST PALO ALTO DIGITAL VILLAGE

It was a rainy, overcast day in East Palo Alto. We all gathered together in a dry conference room, owned by a local community partner. The heat was turned up a little high to take the chill off the unseasonably cold weather outside. All of our jackets and umbrellas were piled on folding chairs by the entrance. There was also plenty of food and coffee to keep us going.

Muki Hansteen-Izora[21] (an African American Stanford graduate student with experience in the community) and I served as the empowerment evaluators. Almost everyone in the room knew each other already, having worked in previous projects in the community. So most of us felt right at home. There was also a halo effect on that day because a cadre of HP leaders were sitting at the table in the room with us. It made us all feel a little more important and assured us that we would be able to accomplish our mission.

HP and the East Palo Alto Digital Village were no strangers. HP was East Palo Alto's biggest corporate brother or sister, funding many community-oriented projects in the past. Whenever HP was involved in a project in the community, they knew it was serious and had a high probability of success associated with it. We were all energized by the influx of cash, equipment, and talent that the Digital Village project represented. We were also excited because our commitment to local control was being validated. HP had made a commitment to allow the community to control both the project and evaluation, and they were honoring it from the very first day.

We started with a few brief introductions to make sure anyone new to the initiative was welcomed. Then we applied the same mission creation process undertaken by the Tribal Digital Village to the East Palo Alto Digital Village. We asked everyone to state what the mission of the East Palo Alto Digital Village was, to record key phrases on a poster sheet in front of the room, and to further discuss what we meant when the posted words did not adequately convey what we meant. The following is a list of some of the key phrases that were generated:

- Empower the community technologically
- Connect organizations and individuals
- Build a sustainable network
- Bridge the digital divide
- Improve the quality of life
- Provide educational and economic benefits
- Develop culturally relevant and appropriate skills and knowledge
- Learners drive and own the learning experience

- Civic engagement and involvement in decision making
- Educate citizens
- Support a continuum of lifelong learning
- Collaborative effort
- Be a part of economic development
- Embrace the diversity of the community

True to form, a pause at the end of the hour resulted in two additional and important contributions:

- Accelerate the pace of positive change
- Be a model for other communities

The race was on. There was no time to drive at the posted speed limit. East Palo Alto Digital Village had an opportunity. They recognized it and seized it. They wanted to accelerate—incremental growth was not an option. In addition, this pause, or moment of reflection, allowed them to think globally—or at least outside their own community. They realized that they were creating a constructive and cohesive model for change. Reflecting on their own values, the community recognized that they had a responsibility and an obligation to share what they were learning and to help other communities leapfrog across their own digital divide.

Muki and one of the community members volunteered to draft a mission statement based on the ideas expressed in those phrases. They shared drafts with members of the Digital Village, revised it based on their comments, and posted it on the Web to help guide the effort. This exercise was useful because it helped to clarify their purpose. One of the early drafts looked like the following:

> To create an informed, connected and empowered community by combining technology, brainpower and collaborative energy. The community partnership comprises schools, businesses, government and local service organizations dedicated to meeting the needs of East Palo Alto Residents.

Similar to the Tribal Digital Village's mission work, this exercise helped shape the exchange and dialogue throughout the project and empowerment evaluation. It made many implicit understandings explicit. It represented a shared, democratically derived product, a test of their abilities to work together, and evidence that a diverse group could cooperate for the common good. This is an important point. Empowerment evaluation is based on shared common interests. African Americans, Latinos, and Pacific Islanders had different and often competing agendas in East Palo Alto. The Digital Village and empowerment evaluation were not designed to make those differences disappear. Instead, the project and the process were designed to help these diverse groups find common ground, to identify common denominators of self-interest. That process began with the creation of a mission that could be shared across (often conflicting) groups in the community.

The exercise in collaboration was acknowledged and celebrated. A new community-based partnership had been forged in a remarkably short period of time. It almost made our heads spin—the simplicity of the process alone made it a marvel. One person said, "This is easy, why didn't we do this a long time ago?"

The moment passed and the group re-engaged. They shifted gears and prepared to take stock, but with a renewed sense of pride, ownership, and responsibility. A simple initial exercise that was conducted under the right conditions (a "safe" brainstorming environment) with the right players present (an inclusive collection of community members) sharpened their resolve. It also focused their eyes on a much larger shared vision of the social good than when they first walked into the room that morning.

BALTIMORE DIGITAL VILLAGE

It was a winter day in Baltimore. The air was cold and crisp and the reception was a little chilly too. By way of background, it is important to understand that this site was different from the others. First, they had such difficulty even getting started that HP preemptively dispatched Deloitte & Touche to conduct a review and to give them some guidance. They completed the review in one week, and the results were primarily negative. They said the Baltimore Digital Village had "tenuous" vertical and horizontal links between programs, inadequate plans, and not enough staff to complete their work. They meant to be helpful, but they only further demoralized the struggling Digital Village.

Second, they were the only Digital Village to have *uninvited* HP from a planned site visit. They had done the unheard of, almost unimaginable—they had uninvited their sponsor. This is not a decision that most consultants or colleagues would recommend when working with a sponsor, especially if you want to retain their support and to maintain a long-term relationship. The Baltimore Digital Village started with a halo effect and in no time were snatching defeat from the jaws of victory. However, Hewlett-Packard was not upset with Deloitte & Touche's findings or offended by the slight snub (at least not after reflecting on it for a few days). They understood. They placed that behavior in context, in order to interpret their behavior appropriately. The Baltimore Digital Village had a recognized degree of difficulty given the community they were working in. In addition, HP realized that the Baltimore Digital Village was not prepared for the visit. They had miscalculated how long it would take to complete the initial planning phase of this project. They did not think they had reached a "respectable place" in terms of what they had promised HP. (This was confirmed by Deloitte & Touche.) A visit at that juncture would have been a waste of time and a potentially further demoralizing event for everyone. The Baltimore Digital Village rescheduled the visit, but our local empowerment evaluation team arrived at their invitation well before HP was granted that privilege.

Judd Antin,[22] an applied anthropology graduate student from the University of Maryland, College Park; Tiphane Waddell, MBA, JD, an African American community empowerment consultant who had worked with local community members; and I were the empowerment evaluators. Judd had brought me up to speed on the situation and told me he was very pleased I was able to attend this particularly challenging meeting with them.

At the Baltimore Digital Village, the sense of local power was healthy, but in retrospect it was not tempered with enough common sense and diplomacy. It embolden them in ways that later became dysfunctional, bordering on an organizational arrogance. This heady power allowed them to turn away other HP recommended and funded resources that might have helped them clarify and solidify their organizational structure at a much early stage in their development. It also made our initial empowerment evaluation foray into their territory a bit more tenuous. However, we had faith in the process and it was justified. They took a vote to determine if they still wanted our assistance, and the majority enthusiastically welcomed our skills. However, a few community members still needed convincing. So the tone was constructive, positive, but cautious and a bit cold, like the weather outside.

We were all seated in a dark boardroom. The Digital Village leaders orchestrated the meeting, beginning with a round of introductions. They provided updates on their work as part of their check-in, which also helped to familiarize us with their efforts. A few members of the community sprinkled their presentations with a little humor. Levity was instrumental in lightening the tone of the room.[23] The empowerment evaluation team repeatedly offered reassurances, ranging from our commitment to the project to our desire to help them. We did not know at the time that we were perceived as an extension of HP and thus suffered from guilt by association. What won the day was our agreement not to share what we were doing with HP until they were ready to have us share that knowledge or information with them. Suddenly, like a ray of sunshine shining though a cloudy sky, the room became a welcoming place. Almost everyone warmed up to one another. Trust was re-established and faith in the process was restored.

This experience sheds light on the tenuous and often fragile nature of these relationships and how important it is to rectify miscommunications, misunderstandings, and misperceptions from the beginning. We followed the same process as the other Digital Villages. The 2001 version of the mission and vision was the following:

> to develop and facilitate the creation of a sustainable e-living community in the East Baltimore Empowerment Zone. To create a digital community in which technology expands collaboration and entrepreneurial opportunities in education, workforce and economic development, community and housing development, and infrastructure and policy.

The Baltimore Digital Village expanded the scope of the mission in December 2003, by adding the following bullet points:

- Bridging the digital divide
- Building a digital and economic infrastructure
- Improving education

- Partnering and leveraging for success
- Serving as a model of economic development
- Empowering the community

It is rare for a group to revise their mission within a year or two, unless there have been dramatic economic or social changes in the community. However, the Baltimore Digital Village decided that it was necessary to expand their mission statement to accurately reflect their rapidly evolving growth. Their refined mission statement was nevertheless consistent with the original, demonstrating that the group had remained on track with its initial intent (Antin, 2005).

CROSS-SITE COMPARISON

Why was there such a difference between the sites when they were all at the starting line? The answer is that they did not start at the same place, they did not drive the same cars, and the capacity of the drivers differed. Members of the Tribal Digital Village and the East Palo Alto Digital Village each had more experience working with other members of their community. They had both received grants in the past from Hewlett-Packard and from other organizations. The Tribal Digital Village consisted of tribes who knew each other before the project started. Similarly, the East Palo Alto community was small, and the social activists associated with the initiative were reasonably cohesive or at least had worked on related projects together in the past. The Tribal Digital Village and the East Palo Alto Digital Village had recognized leaders in the community, ranging from tribal elders to nonprofit directors. They were both focused on the education of their children, on giving them a leg up in the sustainability game. Focusing on their children gave them a shared or common focal point that required an eye toward the long-term future of their communities. The empowerment evaluation teams were stronger in these communities; one co-empowerment evaluator was a Native American professor, and the other was a graduate student with knowledge and experience in the local community (and complete and immediate access to me as a member of the faculty). Although the Baltimore team consisted of highly qualified and supervised members, distance and the absence of a previous working relationship precluded the same level of accessibility.

These "road conditions" markedly contrasted with Baltimore's terrain. They had an ad hoc governance system, diffuse leadership, less experience working together, and significant project delays. HP tried to help them, but the type of assistance they provided was not perceived to be in touch with the community's concerns, constraints, or context (or in this case, their stage of development). It was also communicated at a high level of abstraction, with the result that it further demoralized the Digital Village. The weaknesses of their relationship with HP was compounded by the fact that the Digital Village was viewed as having committed the ultimate faux pas of "slapping the hand that feeds you." Ironically, the Baltimore Digital Village was predominately composed of business, rather than social service, leaders, which one might think would have given them an edge in a small business–oriented enterprise of this nature. Baltimore was trailing behind even before the race had begun. This raises the question not only of whether the Digital Villages were at the same starting line but of whether they were all even in the same race.

CONCLUSION

The mission may take myriad forms, but the process remains the same. It is characterized by an open, inclusive, brainstorming, consensus-building session. It solidifies values and creates a shared vision of the community's future. It sets the stage for every step along the way.

It also demands participation. An inclusive orientation needs to be adopted. Empowerment evaluators enlist a host of time-honored strategies in community organizing circles, ranging from recruiting community leaders to holding community BBQs to attract people. Once they are present, engagement must be cultivated and facilitated in order to become a natural part of the process. For example, during the mission exercise, a community member is selected to help record the brainstorming exercise. This physical, tactile involvement begins the process of cultivating ownership. It can be enhanced by graphic artists but not replaced by them. Cultivating participation is critical to every step of the process; in fact, each step builds on the next in terms of level of engagement, participation, and thus ownership.

The chapters, like the steps of empowerment evaluation, are building blocks. The mission step represents a form of intellectual scaffolding. It is required in order to prepare the mind to engage in meaningful self-assessment and reflection. The next chapter describes how the Digital Villages took stock of where they were, much like a pit stop in a race, with the aim of using their self-assessment to plan for their future.

6 THE PIT STOP: TAKING STOCK

> It's hard to believe we won that race. The car was good in the end,
> but it took us all day to get the adjustments right. On the dirt, you
> only pit once, but we pitted three times today to get the car where
> it needed to be to win the race.
> —Frank Kimmel

The mission exercise helped the Digital Villages to focus their thoughts and core values. The activity was a rite of solidarity[1] for each of the Digital Villages. It helped to create a special bond within each community and forged an unshakable resolve to move forward and to accomplish their objectives. This resolve and resulting confidence were a function of participation—being part of a larger group with the same objectives. The discussion helped build a sense of community[2] by creating a shared vision of the community's dreams for a better life for their families and themselves. As one member of the Digital Village said, "The mission (discussion) kept our 'eyes on the prize.'"[3]

After the mission step and a brief break, each of the Digital Villages launched right into the taking stock exercise. Consisting of a fast-paced diagnostic and repair session, this step was like a pit stop on a racetrack for the Digital Villages. The empowerment evaluation team used the information to design a dashboard and specific gauges, including bar charts and descriptive narratives, to help them monitor their performance while on the track. This rapid appraisal process[4] was designed to minimize time off track, to increase safety (or at least to reduce risk), and to enhance performance. Taking stock helped the Digital Villages to get back on track, moving in the right direction.

TAKING STOCK

Taking stock takes between half a day and a full day to complete. It consists of two steps. The first is for a group to brainstorm[5] about their essential activities and to set priorities—selecting what they think are the most important activities to evaluate as a group. Most members of a group are operating within their comfort zone during this brainstorming step because there are no right or wrong answers. They are simply listing key activities in their organization. These are the activities they perform or monitor on a daily basis. They are familiar with this level of organizational analysis. Many of the ideas that were previously generated during the mission step but were eliminated because they were activities (rather than goals) are now listed in this step. Then the participants are given "sticky dots" to vote for the activities they think need to be evaluated by the group. Some of my colleagues eagerly criticize this step, saying, "That's not very quantitative." My response is always the same, "Count the dots, seems pretty quantitative to me." The activities that receive the most dots get placed on another poster sheet.

The second step is to rate (or to evaluate) how well they are doing and then discuss their assessment. The participants put their initials at the top of their rating column on the poster paper. There is nothing confidential about this process, in part because it is important to hear what people are willing to say within the context of their working environment (which they must return to after this exercise). There is also a functional basis for the initials. It enables the coach to call on each person and ask them why they rated communication, for example, a 3 or a 4 on a 10-point scale. Grounded in the individual's view of their organizational reality, the ratings are an important launching point to engage in dialogue.

The discussion, or dialogue, part of the process is one of the most important elements of the empowerment evaluation process. It is where the rubber meets the road—where real issues are placed on the table and conflicting views of reality about what is really happening collide. I should note that this part of the process is not always smooth, that is, without conflict and miscommunication. In an empowerment evaluation about a teenage pregnancy prevention program in a township in South Africa, one mother asked why we even needed a center, since it presumed premarital sex, which was forbidden in her religion. Another mother hopped up out of her chair, tapped her on the wrist and said, "The reason we need a teenage pregnancy prevention program is because your daughter is pregnant." It was the first time she had heard this news, and as you might imagine, it stopped the process cold. There was yelling, finger-pointing, and the normal stages of anger, denial, shame, and blame.

However, it all took place within the confines of the exercise. Detours were required. Time was devoted to sorting out feelings and finding more diplomatic ways of communicating. If one mother had concerns about the center, others had similar objections. It was important to air these concerns and come to a consensus about the problem and what needed to be done about it. This mother continued to object to the teenage pregnancy prevention program because she thought people *wanted it*. When she realized they *did not want it* but thought the community *needed it*, she understood. After an open discussion of this nature, the exercise continued. Conflict was acknowledged, confronted, and used to construct a healthier understanding of where the group was going. However, it was not allowed to completely derail the process. In other words, the process is not always smooth, but each step has a place for conflict, detours, and moments of agreement before the drivers of the initiative are helped to return to the track.

Overall, taking stock is like seeing your reflection in the pond—for a moment suspended in time, you can see yourself for who you really are before the ripples return to hide your reflection from view.

TRIBAL DIGITAL VILLAGE

The tribes moved from crafting their mission to the taking stock step of the process during the same morning. The tribes recognized that it was not realistic to attempt to evaluate all of their activities, just as it was not realistic or desirable to attempt to evaluate everything in a conventional evaluation. They created a list of the most significant activities that they were engaged in at the time, specifically, those that would help them to accomplish the goals embedded in their mission statement.

One of the most important Tribal Digital Village activities was training youth. They realized that training and socializing the next generation in high tech activities, such as building towers and receiving router training,[6] were the secret to sustainability. The youth represented their hope for the future.

A second critical activity was seeking funding, grants, and other resources to continue their work beyond their Hewlett-Packard funding stream. This is a path most funders value—encouraging the community to pursue the road toward self-help and self-sufficiency.[7] They like to plant the seed by making an initial investment in the community, and then they expect them to continue to grow on their own.[8]

Communication, a universal activity and concern, was the third highest item on their list to evaluate. This one focused on difficulties with internal communication and had implications for external communication with HP and society in general. The remaining activities were focused on specific project activities, ranging from mechanical concerns such as equipment delivery and installation to the larger task of building a wireless network.

The tribes rated how well they were doing as a group in each of these areas, using the 1 (low) to 10 (high) point scale.[9] The top three concerns received fair to middling ratings. For example, youth training received a 4.8 on a 10-point scale. They were pleased with their plans for the youth, including enrolling them in router training—to ensure that they could repair and maintain the wireless system they were building. However, the ratings were not high because only a few students were enrolled in training at the time.

Funding received a similar rating, 5.1, because community's relationship with HP was positive and their funding stream was still going strong. In addition, they were submitting proposals for additional resources from other funding organizations. They realized, however, that they were not exploring enough options to ensure continued support and growth if their current funding streams were to stop flowing.

Communication received middling ratings, 4.8. There was a consensus that although structures were in place to make communication possible, it merited serious attention. Complaints were open and often vociferous about poor communication within the Digital Village. "There is no good communication around here," claimed one tribal member, who thought his tribe had been disenfranchised in terms of tribal services and support. Tribal members asked why some tribes received prompt attention to inquiries about their equipment, while others made repeated requests for a status update and did not receive a response at all. They had to support their views with evidence, such as number of calls made seeking assistance, logs of inquiries and complaints, and equipment manifests and inventories.

These uneven ratings about communication opened the door to a discussion about other communications-related problems that needed to be addressed by the group. For example, there was a community expectation that a computer would be in every home by the middle of the project. However, the Digital Village executive group neglected to inform community members of their plan of action, which was to build the network first and then deliver the computers to every home. Had they shared this internal plan with the community earlier for additional consideration, expectations might have been in line with their plan. Alternatively, they may have modified their plan and respected the wishes of community members who wanted to have the computers first so they would have time to become more familiar with them before they were connected to the Internet. This misstep was useful. It highlighted the importance of consulting with the community at every step and not assuming that any group "knows what's best for the entire community." It also served to emphasize why ongoing communication (including managing expectations) about implementation is critical. It was an early and important "lessons learned." It was also a good example of single loop learning, addressing a specific problem in order to keep things on track concerning the existing plans.

The benefits of this particular discussion kept flowing. Delays in equipment delivery were initially viewed as problems resulting from poor communication within the reservation boundaries. However, as the evidence was examined, the root of the problem did not reside within the reservation. It was HP's problem. It was an unanticipated by-product of the merger between HP and Compaq[10] that slowed down production and equipment delivery schedules. It was a memorable "aha"[11] moment that the group experienced during this dialogue about the ratings. A few calls and emails were made to other Digital Villages to confirm that this problem was systemic. In the process, an informal link was created between the Digital Village sites (an unanticipated positive outcome associated with this problem). It resulted in double loop learning organizationally because it created an entirely new dimension to communication—cross Digital Village communication—which prompted HP to re-think its entire communication strategy for the project. Eventually it produced a centralized repository for Digital Village knowledge. Although it was created late in the project, some Digital Villages grew and developed exponentially in large part due to this centralized Digital Village database.

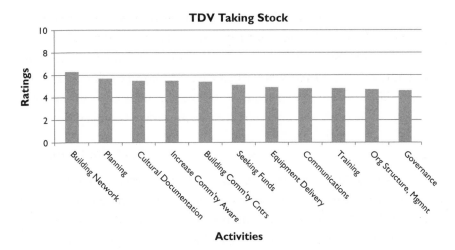

FIGURE 5. Tribal Digital Village's baseline taking stock ratings.

Ironically, building the actual network received high ratings, 6.3, mostly because they were building the towers and laying the lines with their own hands. They were very analytical about the process. For example, they were able to separate equipment delivery issues, which received a low 4.9 rating, from the building of the actual network, which received a 6.3. Instead of commingling the impact equipment delivery was having on building the network, they treated them as two separate (but related) activities. This enabled them to once again focus on the areas in need of attention while they recognized the gains made overall. (See Figure 5 for a summary of their assessments across all activities.)

EAST PALO ALTO DIGITAL VILLAGE

The East Palo Alto Digital Village followed the same format as the Tribal Digital Village, quickly shifting gears from establishing their mission to taking stock in the same day. This exercise in setting priorities was revealing. As might be expected in a community-based initiative, communication,[12] collaboration,[13] fund-raising,[14] capacity building,[15] and training[16] were paramount. These are the classic ingredients of a strong initiative. They are also the most common reasons for failure. The community had accurately identified the critical underlying variables associated with their endeavor.

The list of activities that the group generated but did not assign any dots to was equally interesting and insightful, such as leadership development, establishing standard operating procedures, dissemination of the initiative, and governance. These activities were important enough to add to the list of critical activities, but they were not considered the most important ones for the group to focus on as a group at that time. In some cases, they also knew some of these activities would be handled by other parties and leaders they trusted and thus they were not important enough to take the time and resources of the entire group (at that stage of the group's development). Sometimes the rationale for their choices was just common sense. They had to get things in motion and to begin to operate before they could worry about establishing *standard operating procedures.*

Once again they used their judgment wisely in recognizing that they only had so much energy, and while these activities were important, other matters took precedence at that time. Empowerment evaluation provided them with a tool to make this decision, but it was the group consensus and wisdom that guided the initiative at that juncture in its development and evolution.

The East Palo Alto Digital Village members rated each of the high-priority activities, using the same 1 (low) to 10 (high) point scale as the other Digital Villages. They rated how well they were doing as a group concerning each of these activities.[17] This provided a baseline assessment of where the group thought they were on each of the activities. A baseline is critical because it provides a starting point from which to measure growth over time. (See Figure 6 for an abbreviated depiction of their ratings.)

The group rated themselves highest in the areas of program development and management (implementation). Their lowest ratings were for fund-raising, client case management, and communication. The dialogue generated from these numbers was not always calm, but it was evidence based. It was not evidence-based practice[18] (Cochrane, 1972; Melnyk and Fineout-Overholt, 2005), which typically requires a statistical significance of effectiveness, but practice-based evidence (Gabbay and LeMay, 2011), which relies heavily on context and common sense. Everyone had to provide a basis for their opinions or ratings. This helped to build a culture of evidence, which became a norm at subsequent gatherings. More to the point, it helped the group be-

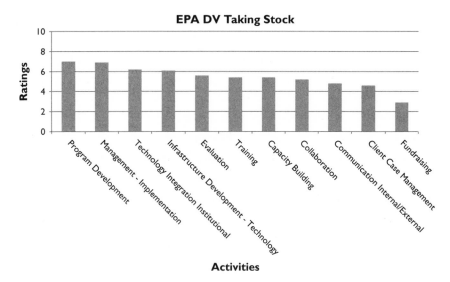

FIGURE 6. East Palo Alto Digital Village's baseline taking stock ratings.

come more precise and efficient in its use of resources. The reasons for the rating helped to pinpoint the solution. For example, fund-raising was rated poorly. The evidence included the absence of a plan to raise funds, the lack of grant writing, no effort to reach prospective funders, no follow-up to leverage existing funding relationships (including with HP), and inadequate efforts to monetize existing products. Instead of using up precious time and resources brainstorming about fund-raising, the East Palo Alto Digital Village had come up with a more refined plan directly related to what they viewed as the problem (or the basis for their low ratings for funding).

BALTIMORE DIGITAL VILLAGE

The Baltimore Digital Village's Executive Committee used their mission exercise as a launching pad to generate a list of BDV's critical activities. The top ten items on their list, according to the BDV Executive Committee, included fund-raising, transferring ownership of the initiative to the community, and disseminating technology throughout the community. These were logical choices and all tied to their mission.

After setting priorities for the most significant activities, they rated how well they were doing.[19] They were extremely self-critical. None of the ratings were above a 4 on a 10-point scale. They knew they were in trouble on almost every front. They gave themselves the lowest ratings for fund-raising, public relations and marketing efforts, leveraging resources, and transferring ownership to the community. They were having difficulty financially, getting their message across about what they were about, and giving their power away. This is significant because transferring power to the community, cultivating a sense of ownership, and allowing community members to take responsibility for Digital Village activities is at the heart of the community-based project.

Their highest score was assigned to setting project priorities. They knew they were in trouble and unable to address this problem, but they gave themselves a high rating to acknowledge the amount of time they had devoted to the task. It had consumed more time and energy than any other task on their plate. It was an ironic rating because problems in setting priorities for their tasks were the reason in large part for inviting the empowerment evaluators to assist them. They were not deluded. They just were not successful at it because they were still competing with each other internally (protecting their pet projects) instead of cooperating as part of a unified group with a larger vision. In any case, even their highest ratings were below a 4 on a 10-point scale. (See Figure 7 for their ratings.)

These foundational insights and understandings grounded the Baltimore Digital Village. They also served a secondary purpose. They helped prepare the Baltimore Digital Village to interpret and appreciate Deloitte & Touche's earlier comments. Deloitte & Touche's review was not bad or wrong. They were very bright, experienced professionals. However, their review was not aimed at the Baltimore Digital Village's stage of development or entrepreneurial and managerial level of sophistication. It was aimed at a more mature level of organizational and managerial development. In addition, the language of the review was at a much higher level of abstraction than was appropriate for members of the Digital Village. Thus at the time the Deloitte & Touche reviewers were perceived as irrelevant, insulting, and discouraging. Now "horizontal and vertical links between programs" made sense. The critique about "inadequate plans" was obvious in retrospect. "Insufficient staffing" now was inter-

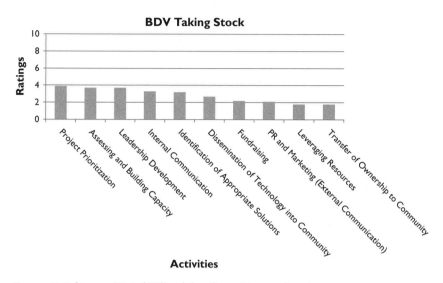

FIGURE 7. Baltimore Digital Village's baseline taking stock ratings.

preted as the need to request and/or deploy more resources rather than as an opportunity to play the "blame and shame" game. This change in outlook represented an excellent example of how internal and external evaluations need not be mutually exclusive. They can complement each other and enhance each other, as long as the external evaluation is rooted in internal concerns and aimed at the developmentally appropriate level.

Taking stock allowed the Baltimore Digital Village to stop racing and to reflect on its experience enough to hear their coach's comments. A racing coach of mine once told me if you are racing at 100 percent of your capacity you can not hear anything because you are holding on for dear life. Sometimes it is important to drive at 80 percent of your capacity so that you can take in the comments and criticisms and do something about it. Sometimes you simply have to stop or, more precisely, to slow down. This is what taking stock is all about.

CROSS-SITE COMPARISON

The Tribal Digital Village and the East Palo Alto Digital Village were still in the lead. They started with a competitive advantage. The Tribal Digital Village knew where they wanted to go. They were training their youth technologically and in the process socializing the next generation. The translation was simple: towers and routers were going to be their secret to sustainability. It gave them a long-term focus with the simultaneous need to focus on the immediate, the here and now—their children. This was a generalizable capacity that helped them in every other dimension of the construction of their Digital Village. In addition, they continued to maintain a healthy relationship with their sponsor, were seeking out other funding sources, and were able to confront communication problems early on before tribal communication imploded.

The East Palo Alto Digital Village had the same kinds of advantages. They had a handle on the classic ingredients of strong initiatives, including communication, collaboration, fund-raising, capacity building, and training. They also had a healthy relationship with HP and were becoming aware of their branding and communication issues. This helped them stay on track with a purpose and a place to go.

The Baltimore Digital Village used the taking stock exercise to take a hard cold look at themselves. They were very self-critical. They knew they were in trouble, but the taking stock exercise helped them crystallize what they knew already, even if it was only an emergent understanding of the seriousness of their place in the race. It also helped them to begin to appreciate the earlier advice they had received from Deloitte & Touche but were not ready to receive at the time and in the tone it was delivered.

The taking stock exercise also helped to level the playing field. It made each of them stop in their tracks and look at themselves. The Tribal Digital Village saw where they were, and it helped them project where they would be in the future if they stayed on the same path. What they saw spurred them on to continue to expand their funding streams and confront communication problems head on. The East Palo Alto Digital Village used this tool to bring their funding and communication issues up front, which motivated them to address these issues. The Baltimore Digital Village saw their shortcomings and knew it was time to make a change and begin listening to people who were trying to help them. The taking stock exercise did not eliminate the advantages or disadvantages they started with, but it did help them take a hard look at their position on the track. The taking stock exercise helped each of them prepare for the next lap in the race of their lives.

CONCLUSION

These brief presentations demonstrate why taking stock is so important to the process. The ratings represented a shorthand way of expressing satisfaction (or dissatisfaction) with program implementation and progress. In addition, they were a springboard for discussion about community issues and concerns. Dialogue is one of the most important parts of an empowerment evaluation. It is during these exchanges that people provide their rationale and evidence for their ratings. This discussion helps to identify where the group needs to put its efforts during the planning for the future stage—and thus saves time and energy.

Instead of postulating about a series of solutions that were not linked to the groups' concerns and complaints (or stage of development) at the time, a common error in strategic planning, the groups were able to focus on precisely the matters that concerned them. They focused on the obstacles and challenges that formed the basis for their low ratings. Similarly, they were able to build on strengths by specifying what worked, namely, the activities that received high ratings.

They were also able to engage in single and double loop learning. Single loop learning was more common as Digital Village community members brainstormed about ways to improve program performance. However, there was no shortage of double loop learning because everything was so new. It was like the number of epiphanies a teenager has every week. They slow down and become few and far between as we become older and have been desensitized to the wonder of what we now consider routine. Similarly, the number of "aha" moments for the Digital Villages were more frequent at the beginning of the process, but the quality of them improved over time as the groups learned to work together and to understand the issues of development in greater depth.

Taking stock, like the mission step, requires participation. Now, however, the conceptual and physical level of involvement is escalated, as is the sense of ownership. Now people are putting their views on the line. It is one thing to talk about one's dreams during the mission step, where there is less at stake. It is a completely different matter when one must pinpoint areas for review and judgment and provide reasons for one's assessments. The taking stock step is where participants put it on the line.

This "putting it on the line" also applies to the mechanics of conducting an empowerment evaluation as well. It might be easier and more efficient for the empowerment evaluator to record the priority dots and rating scores themselves by simply entering them into their laptop. However, there is something almost magical about people physically placing their dots and ratings on the poster paper before the entire community that binds them to those views and consequently creates a commitment to doing something about them. The level of participation and engagement on every level is escalated from mission to taking stock.

Taking stock was like being a member of a race car's pit crew. The Digital Village community and the empowerment evaluators rapidly inspected the project—a vehicle for social justice. Critical gauges and instruments, including bar charts and verbatim quotations, were monitored. The information gained from this exercise helped us to pinpoint the reasons for high and low ratings. The reasons provided the group not only with an insight into what the relevant community issues were but with the knowledge to solve or to build on them. The dialogue provided the group with the information they needed to anticipate the future and thus enabled community members to see ahead of the curve of social change. This step became the basis for the next step of the process—planning for the future.

7 BACK ON THE TRACK:

PLANNING FOR THE FUTURE OR

IMPLEMENTING AN INNOVATION

Circumstances may cause interruptions and delays, but never
lose sight of your goal. Prepare yourself in every way you can by
increasing your knowledge and adding to your experiences, so
that you can make the most of an opportunity when it occurs.
—Mario Andretti

Empowerment evaluation shifts into high gear at the planning for the future stage, whereas most conventional forms of evaluation are idling or have finished the race. I am often asked at the beginning of an empowerment evaluation, "What tools do you need to conduct an empowerment evaluation?," and my response is always, "I don't know." At least I don't know all of them. I know they need to establish a mission and take stock of where they are. I also know, as part of planning for the future, that the community needs to specify goals and to generate strategies to accomplish them. They also need to agree (with their funders) upon credible evidence to support their assessments. This is all part of an implicit logic model[1] or program theory,[2] in essence explaining how the Digital Village is supposed to work with various inputs and outputs, goals and outcomes. However, there is no way of knowing what evaluation tools are needed until the community's plans for the future are unveiled. The plans for the future represent the intervention[3] in evaluation language. Once we knew what the plans for the future were in each of the Digital Villages, we were able to help them select the most appropriate methodological tools, such as online surveys, observations, document review, and ethnographic methods (Fetterman, 2010). They used these tools to monitor and to assess their performance. If we had selected the tools before we knew what their plans for the future were, we would have been guilty of allowing the methodological tail to wag the evaluation dog.

The shifts from crafting a mission to taking stock to planning for the future is a process of reduction. When cooking, the amount of liquid or sauce in the pan is reduced by boiling it. When the liquid evaporates you are left with the essentials: a concentrated sauce and an enhanced flavor. The same conceptual process was used by the Digital Villages. Reduction helped the communities to narrow their focus on the most relevant issues and to select the most meaningful indicators to determine if they were addressing their problems.

Empowerment evaluation also concentrates and focuses energy. It is like a magnifying glass focusing the sun's light on a piece of paper. With the aid of a magnifying glass, a tiny spot of sunlight shining on a piece of paper can start a fire. Without the magnifying glass, the sunlight is too diffuse to produce a flame. Empowerment evaluation, like a magnifying glass, helps to concentrate the efforts of the group. It provided a mechanism for the Digital Villages to establish shared goals and activities. In the process, it helped them to use their limited resources more wisely, efficiently, and expeditiously. Reduction and concentration in the empowerment evaluation process can produce a recipe for success and ignite a community into action.

PLANNING FOR THE FUTURE

The planning for the future exercise is brief. It takes between a few hours to a full day to complete, depending on the size of the group and the scope of the issues. It is typically held a day or a week after the taking stock exercise to give people enough time to absorb the experience, but not enough time to forget and to lose the momentum between the exercises. Although the exercise is brief, the cycle of planning, implementing, evaluating, revising implementation plans, and assessing implementation continues ad infinitum.

Planning for the future begins by establishing goals. The goals are related to the activities rated and discussed in the taking stock step. If fund-raising, for example, was rated and discussed during taking stock, a goal concerning fund-raising would be proposed in the planning for the future step. The goal would be simple: to improve fund raising efforts. Typically, a group only selects three goals to begin with, otherwise the effort becomes overwhelming, diffused, and diluted. Over time the group can continue to add new goals, based on the activities assessed in the taking stock step.

The empowerment evaluator asks members of the community to suggest strategies to accomplish their goals. The strategies are rooted in the taking stock dialogue or exchange. The strategies are suggested by members of the community rather than by an external expert. The coach might periodically make a suggestion or two but does not dominate the discussion or session. The coach asks, however, what kind of evidence would be credible to determine if the strategies are working. In particular, two kinds of evidence are solicited: (1) that which determines if the strategies are being implemented and (2) that which determines if the strategies are effective in accomplishing the group's goals.

Planning for the future is not conducted in a vacuum. It is conducted within the real world, within the context of accountability or what the group is held accountable for already. Real-world constraints do not disappear. It is within this zone, on the one hand, that the importance of compliance and commitments are acknowledged. This level of accountability gives the entire enterprise additional credibility. On the other hand, it is the illusion of stability created by these rules and requirements that allows for creativity, deviation from the norm, and new ways of doing things to emerge. The Digital Villages were traveling in unchartered territory. They benefited from having goals, concrete strategies, and measureable outcomes. The unpredictability of the path within this framework is where necessity became the mother of invention.

TRIBAL DIGITAL VILLAGE

The tribes developed their plans for the future based on their self-assessment or taking stock exercise. They were, in essence, designing and constructing their own conceptual building blocks. Training youth, seeking funding for sustainability,[4] communication, and increasing community awareness were the most significant areas addressed during the taking stock step. Consequently, those became the same activities used to inform their plans for the future.

TRAINING YOUTH

Training youth received a moderate rating by the Tribal Digital Village. They acknowledged and even celebrated their accomplishments, but recognized that there was tremendous room for improvement. Their goal was simple: to improve training and to train more youth. A few of their strategies included the following:

- increasing the number of youth enrolled in Cisco router training;
- providing youth with training and apprenticeship opportunities, specifically helping to build the towers;
- recruiting youth to recruit more youth (peer recruitment); and
- asking for youth views about the training (using the data to refine training practices).

The evidence was both quantitative and qualitative.[5] They established a baseline,[6] counting the number of youth already enrolled in various training programs. Then they counted the number of new youth who had enrolled in router repair classes and participated in apprenticeship opportunities after their campaign to increase their numbers. Peer to peer recruitment proved to be effective. They also observed the technical training sessions and asked participating youth to comment on the quality of instruction. Their feedback was used to revamp both the curricular content and the instructional style. It made the classes more relevant and meaningful to them, which helped to retain matriculating students and to attract a new cohort of youthful trainees.

FUNDING

One of Tribal Digital Village's top priorities was to seek additional funding for sustainability. This translated into a series of interrelated mini-goals. They were determined to secure enough money to train more people, particularly youth. They wanted to assure the community that the Digital Village would continue to generate an ongoing funding stream to support a host of activities on the reservation. Thus they made a commitment to stimulate economic development across the reservations and to become an economically sustainable enterprise (see Figure 8).

The empowerment evaluation process encourages communities to generate their own strategies to accomplish their goals. One of the Tribal Digital Village strategies included planning to operate a for-profit digital printing press.[7] This

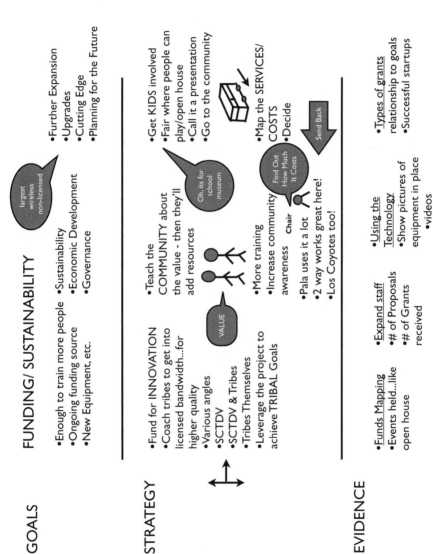

FIGURE 8. Graphic artist's depiction of the dialogue about funding (redrawn for publication).

was one way to stimulate economic development, to make the Digital Village an economically sustainable enterprise, and to create an ongoing funding stream. Another strategy was to create a wireless network.[8]

The Tribal Digital Village also implemented a micro-strategy that paid off immediately. They created a funding map. With the assistance of HP leadership, they drew a chart depicting the amount of money dedicated to each major activity (see Figure 9). For example, of the $5 million grant, approximately

- $2.5 million was already spent on equipment;
- $1 million was already spent on personnel and building the network; and
- $1 million was already set aside for new tribal business.

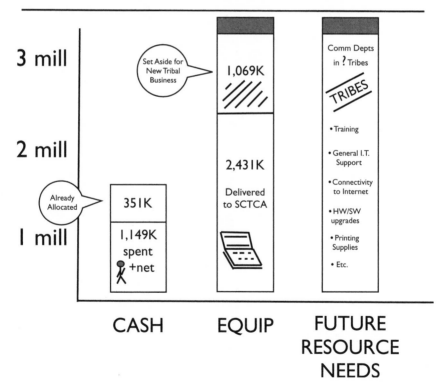

FIGURE 9. Funding map (redrawn for publication).

This left the Digital Village with less than a half million dollars to complete their objectives and to create a self-sustaining operation. This simple funding map created a sense of urgency that motivated the tribes to accelerate their pace and to shift their plans into high gear. Grant writing became a higher priority and resulted in substantial and ongoing revenue streams for the tribes.

The evidence they relied on to document their success included writing and securing million dollar grants,[9] operating their own digital printing press, and launching their own wireless network. Each one of these has tremendous face validity. In other words, just by looking at these accomplishments, they could see they were successful in reaching their goals.

Monitoring and evaluating these goals did not require methodological sophistication because the accomplishments loomed large. Traditional evaluation tools were useful, however, to help refine and improve performance. Grants were reviewed to determine if they might be used to leverage additional funds from similar agencies and funding sources. Online surveys were created to gauge customer satisfaction with the digital printing press and wireless network operations.

COMMUNICATION

Communication is a universal phenomenon. It is how people share what they know, learn about their environment, make decisions, and execute transactions. Every organization relies on communication to function. Periodically, organizational communications break down.[10] At minimum they do not always function in an optimal fashion. The Tribal Digital Village was no different in this regard. They reported problems communicating both internally and externally. Their goal, simply put, was to improve communications.

They built on their taking stock discussions and immediately instituted logs of all requests and complaints. This enabled individual tribes to track the Digital Village's response time concerning requests for technical assistance. They also established communication protocols, proposal tracking systems, and produced more informative web pages for the community. All of these strategies were rooted in the taking stock discussion and thus represented targeted and surgical interventions. They were responsive to problems pinpointed

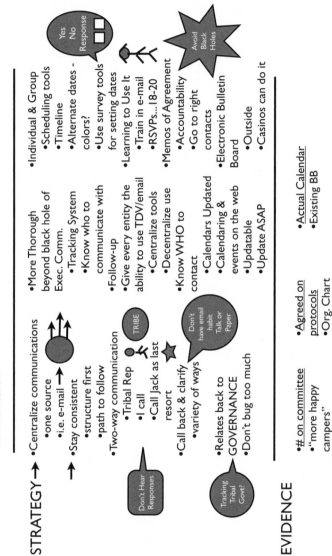

FIGURE 10. Graphic artist's depiction of the dialogue about communication (redrawn for publication).

by the group instead of randomly brainstorming or recruiting an external expert with a solution in search of a problem (see Figure 10).

Evidence of effectiveness was easy to collect. Tribal members were surveyed and interviewed to determine if they were aware of the new protocols, tracking systems, logs, and improved community webpage. Logs were inspected and reviewed. The number of complaints were recorded and counted to determine their frequency before and after new communication strategies were implemented. The result of these efforts was not surprising: complaints about protocols and responsiveness initially increased because new channels of communication had been opened. It was ironic. The Tribal Digital Village was being inundated with input as a result of its own successful strategies to encourage community communication. However, over time the number of basic complaints dwindled, and more sophisticated concerns replaced them. The Digital Village's success in creating a transparent operation and in making information and decisions more accessible to the community solved one problem and created another—a problem many would be happy to have.

EAST PALO ALTO DIGITAL VILLAGE

Whereas the Tribal Digital Village had detailed, concrete plans for the future aimed at ensuring long-term sustainability, East Palo Alto was primarily concerned about how they would continue funding their work in the immediate future. Their HP funding was coming to an end in six months, and they had not acted on their plans for this fiscal transition. They were not ready to operate as an economically viable enterprise on their own. They needed to secure another funding stream. In essence, they needed more time. They were scrambling.

The group used the planning for the future step to reassert itself and re-establish its community-wide commitment to seeking funding. An unanticipated impact of the funding crisis was that it was liberating.[11] It opened the door to re-visiting and re-visioning the mission and the purpose of the group.

The mission became more narrowly focused on being a catalyst and a technical support system for small business, entrepreneurial development, and a communication hub for the community. Their revised goal was simple: find

funding to keep their doors open. Their strategies included leveraging existing partners, including Cisco and local foundations, identifying prospective
funders, and writing grants. They worked at a frenzied pace. These enterpris-
ing efforts were successful in catapulting additional strategies in motion,
ranging from marketing to monetizing existing services. It was as if someone
had lit a match under their feet. They were focused and determined. They used
the same empowerment evaluation formula as the other Digital Villages, creating goals, specifying strategies, and agreeing on credible evidence to document progress toward their goals and objectives. They also introduced another
measure of accountability into the process. They specified who in the group
would be responsible for each new goal and corresponding set of strategies.
This was important because in the past when they had not designated a specific person for each major task, little progress was made and important tasks
would simply slip through the organizational cracks.

After this practice was instituted, members of the East Palo Alto Digital Village were called on by name to report on their subgroup's progress. In addition
to adding a measure of individual accountability, this process helped to institu-
tionalize evaluation. Evaluation updates became a routine part of their meeting
agenda. They made evaluation an integral part of their planning and management. They were engaged in triple loop learning as an organization. It was late
in the game, but they got it. It took a crisis for them to reach this organizational
level of understanding, but they made evaluation an authentic part of their
normal day-to-day decision making. Empowerment evaluation had truly become a useful tool to guide them.

They had no difficulty securing a consensus about the evidence they used to
determine whether they were accomplishing their objectives—money continued to come in and the programs continued to operate and serve the community. There was no need for complex studies of statistical significance.[12] The
outcomes had face validity[13] and were unequivocally persuasive. The East Palo
Alto Digital Village continued to operate and to help their local community
bridge the digital divide.

Communication

It was no accident that communication was right up there with funding. They knew, from their taking stock exercise, that they had not done a good job of communicating their mission. East Palo Alto Digital Village leaders knew that most citizens in the community had no idea what the Digital Village was or what it was doing. The East Palo Alto Digital Village did not have a sufficiently clear and simple message. Their branding (Lindstrom, 2010a, 2010b, 2011) was inconsistent. This was in large part the basis for much of their difficulties. Their efforts to refine the mission helped guide and refocus their communication strategies. (It also demonstrated how interrelated each of the activities were.)

They re-set their strategy priorities, shifting from a one-way communication pattern (from the East Palo Alto Digital Village to the rest of the community) to a two-way line of communication. They provided more opportunities for the community to shape the direction of the East Palo Alto Digital Village. They used community input to inform their program implementation strategies.

The funding crisis helped them to be more accountable internally and externally. They streamlined their message in order to be more responsive to community concerns. The East Palo Alto Digital Village literally opened up portals to facilitate community conversation and communication. They made the East Palo Alto Digital Village webpage more accessible. They made it a one-stop shopping site, where community members could send and receive their email, learn about important community events and services, surf the net, and post their ideas about social and economic reform initiatives in the community.

They relied on community webpage-use statistics, online community surveys, and media coverage of East Palo Alto Digital Village activities to monitor and to assess the effectiveness of their services and their marketing campaign. They turned the operation around just in the nick of time. Community support led to local political support. This in turn helped convince funders that the East Palo Alto Digital Village was still vital and thus would prove a good investment for the long-term health of the community.

BALTIMORE DIGITAL VILLAGE

The Baltimore Digital Village was the least prepared of the Digital Villages for the transition to independence and self-sufficiency. They readily acknowledged this state of affairs. They also knew they needed help. They knew they had a finite amount of time and money remaining before their funding would end. Their first goal was to set priorities for their projects with the aim of focusing on their most promising initiatives or at least identifying the ones with the most immediate payoff. They applied the same taking stock exercise to this task and successfully set priorities for their projects in less than an hour—a task they had been unable to accomplish in the preceding years.

They agreed to focus on tech support packages for small businesses. The packages typically included all-in-one fax/photocopier/scanner/printer equipment and digital cameras. They also included computer and Internet training. The packages were designed to provide local entrepreneurs and small businesses with tech tools that would help them to innovate, to be more efficient, and to be more profitable. Before this point, the Baltimore Digital Village was all over the map, spreading itself thin, and accomplishing little in any of its major intervention areas. This simplified message and service was understood and welcomed in the community. It helped them turn their efforts around.

Applying the process to communication, they were able to open up new lines of communication with HP as well. This time, however, communication would not include uninviting a sponsor. Their success in these areas encouraged them to address other important concerns that consumed the other Digital Villages, such as fund-raising.

These small wins, their additional experience building the Digital Village, and the time devoted to taking stock of their progress bolstered their confidence. It prepared them to mine existing resources. For example, the Deloitte & Touche report resurfaced. They used parts of the report that now made sense to them in their business blueprint for action. One indicator of their shift in self-confidence was that their jokes were redirected at themselves, instead of Deloitte & Touche or HP. This was an indirect measure of their organizational and managerial maturity.

The Baltimore Digital Village was well on its way to turning its operation around. However, it still had not addressed a basic institutional liability. They were an Executive Committee. They were not a 501(c)3 nonprofit or other unified organizational entity. They lacked institutional stability, which made supervisory and leadership transitions organizational mine fields. It also jeopardized their ability to attract future funding and thus their sustainability.

CROSS-SITE COMPARISON

Some of the Digital Village leaders were falling asleep at the wheel. The taking stock exercise helped to wake them up. The Tribal Digital Village celebrated their accomplishments but recognized there was room for improvement even in areas where they were making progress. From their perspective, they were falling short of their ambitious goals. The East Palo Alto Digital Village and the Baltimore Digital Village considered the findings of their taking stock exercise to be a wake-up call. Both needed to focus on funding immediately to stay in the race.

Planning for the future helped each one of them in remarkably similar ways, respecting and reflecting their very different individual stages of development. The Tribal Digital Village was clearly in the lead and in the fast lane. However, they could not afford to do everything and still reach their goals. This tool helped them focus on a delimited number of initiatives including recruiting more youth to enroll in router training, designing a blueprint for their digital printing press operations, continuing to build the towers for their wireless network, and diversifying their funding stream.

The East Palo Alto Digital Village was scrambling to stay in the race. Their funding was less secure than that of the Tribal Digital Village but more secure than that of the Baltimore Digital Village. The scope of their market plan and mission had to be reduced. The planning for the future exercise helped them to do precisely that at a time when it was most needed. It helped keep them solvent and in fact energized their entire operations.

The Baltimore Digital Village had stalled. They were almost out of the race. They were not ready to transition to a self-sufficient proposition. They used the planning for the future exercise to set priorities for their projects (their business portfolio), refocus their mission, and streamline their services. The planning for the future exercise simultaneously built up their confidence and "gave them permission" to mine existing (but previously neglected) resources, such as the Deloitte & Touche report.

All three Digital Villages used the planning for the future exercise to improve communication. The Tribal Digital Village used this approach to improve their internal communication. The East Palo Alto and Baltimore Digital Villages used it to improve their branding and external communication, which strengthened their capacity to serve their respective community. While taking stock helped them take a good look at themselves, planning for the future gave them a way to do something about what they saw. It was clear that the Digital Villages were not racing against each other. In some respects they were not even in the same race. They were racing against themselves. Planning for the future fueled their efforts to continue moving forward and to finish their own race to the finish line.

CONCLUSION

Planning for the future represents one step (not the final step) in the infinite loop of implementing and evaluating in empowerment evaluation. Plans for the future were the Digital Villages' intervention. This step represents the implementation of an innovation. It is when thoughts, ideas, and dreams are implemented and turned into functioning realities. Johnson (2010) calls this space where "good ideas come from" the "liquid network." These dreams were rooted in their self-assessments of their own program performance, which were rooted in their mission or core values. The implementations of the Digital Villages' strategies were monitored and evaluated. The data were used to inform decision making concerning program operations, ranging from summative go/no-go decisions to formative refinements and improvements.[14]

Adding Wings to Ideas

It is one thing to dream about dreams, which is much of what the mission exercise is all about. It is another thing all together to begin to give that dream feet to walk on, grounding it in our daily lives. That is what taking stock helps people accomplish. Planning for the future represents an entirely separate dimension. It is when people add wings to their ideas and let their dreams fly.

Learning to fly requires being present in the moment—it requires immersion, attention, focus, dedication, and ongoing participation. This is what makes planning for the future ideas a reality. It is about community and program staff members generating goals, strategies, and credible evidence. It is about implementing those strategies, monitoring, assessing, and feeding it all back into their daily practice.

In the process, people are putting their ideas, reputations, and pride on the line before their families and the entire community. They learn to take responsibility for specific group goals for the organization. Taking responsibility for publically reporting on progress in each area adds a measure of accountability to the endeavor and once again escalates responsibility and subsequently ownership.

Many evaluators and community organizers might jump in at this point and think they could conduct the evaluation more efficiently themselves, ranging from setting the goals to collecting the data. They may be correct, but do they live in the community? Are they going to stay there, long after the project has come and gone? Community members need to learn how to monitor and assess their own program. There are times when it is important not to be efficient, and this is one of them. For evaluators and community organizers to jump in would be a false efficiency. Doing so robs people of agency and responsibility, minimizes motivation, and undermines their participation. It closes the window of opportunity to create an environment that is conducive to cultivating empowerment.

One of my own missteps helps to illustrate this point. During an empowerment evaluation at Stanford University's Lucille Packard Children's Hospital, I made the mistake of assigning planning for the future goals to individuals and asking them to return to the next session with detailed plans. They came back and no one agreed with anyone else's proposed goals, strategies, or evidence. We did not have any agreement and thus no buy-in. We had to repeat this exercise as a group and come to a consensus about what we all thought were appropriate goals, strategies, and evidence. It was important for me as the empowerment evaluator to step back and to allow the participants to be as inefficient as possible in the short run, so that they could embrace the spirit of efficiency in the long run.

Applying the Brakes to Win the Race

The planning for the future exercise helped the Digital Villages learn how to apply the brakes in order to win the race. On the street, you brake incrementally when going into a curve. Most programs see an obstacle and follow this same approach. They slow down. It seems reasonable but it the wrong thing to do. Time is something you can't replace. It is often lost as a result of fear, indecision, and hesitation.

In a race you drive as fast as you can and then brake fast. You don't slam on your breaks and overcorrect your steering. This will result in a tailspin, which in the spirit of full disclosure I have done while racing with Ferraris.[15] Instead, you drive as fast as your ability permits and brake at the last possible moment. You do not waste any time this way. This allows you to successfully negotiate the turn in the most efficient manner, whether it is a failing business plan, a fiscal or operational obstacle, or a pivotal decision to expand or to diversify operations. These are things that have to be faced, dealt with, and left behind.

The financial mapping plan was a form of braking that helped motivate the Tribal Digital Village. They could see how little money was left in the buckets. It pushed them to apply for and to secure more grants than anticipated, to finish building the towers on time, and to open the printing press for business in a timely manner. Applying the brakes helped the East Palo Alto Digital Village to narrow its scope and to focus on providing technical support for business development. Similarly, the Baltimore Digital Village braked to set priorities for its portfolio of projects, focusing on the ones with the greatest payoff. The issue of institutional stability was raised explicitly during the planning for the future exercise. However, the institutional liability never negotiated the curve. They delayed again, failing to confront the issue and to make a decision about their organizational status. They needed to speed toward the corner (or decision) and brake fast (and act). In other words, they needed to confront the issue head on. Their institutional stability issue resulted in an organizational tailspin.

Learning that braking was just as important to speed as using the throttle put the Digital Villages through their paces. They kept racing along the track with their program implementation. At the last possible moment, before the funding stream was about to dry up, they applied the brakes. They narrowed their focus and sharpened their marketing plans. Then they accelerated out of the curve, implementing the new, more narrowly devised "business plans." Braking correctly positioned their organizations on the track in a way that not only carried more speed into the corner but placed the Digital Villages in a position that allowed them to generate the fastest exit speed—and that's how each of them won the race.

The planning for the future exercises were instrumental to the survival and the sustainability of the Digital Villages. All of the Digital Villages needed to stop what they were doing and re-think their "business plan." The money was running out, and they could not just keep on racing down the track in a business as usual fashion. They had to devise a new racing strategy, and this step gave them a tool to do precisely that.

Planning for the future does take hard work. However, empowerment evaluation, particularly during the planning for the future step, does not feel like work once you are immersed in it. You enter a zone, like driving on a track, lap after lap. For hours, you live in a world of your own, racing against yourself. Time no longer exists. It is the flow that Csíkszentmihályi et al. (2005) speaks about when you are productively focused in a successful engagement. You are motivated, energized, and on a mission. In essence, just because it looks like hard work doesn't mean it needs to be. As Thomas Edison said, "Opportunity is missed by most people because it is dressed in overalls, and looks like work."[16]

Empowerment evaluation, however, is not a panacea. It did not solve all the Digital Villages' problems. What empowerment evaluation did was to help them feed what they learned about their operations back into their daily practice. Knowledge is power, and the Digital Villages decided to make use of this power. They used empowerment evaluation to become their own learning organizations.[17]

Learning organizations, however, like other organizations, have to produce results within real-world time constraints. They need to meet deadlines. The success of the Digital Village learning organization was dependent on their attentiveness to the clock as it kept ticking. They had to deliver and on a schedule. The way to do this was to measure change over time—to see what they were accomplishing and on what schedule—as a result of their practice-based, evidence-driven decisions and actions. The next chapter is about the organizational stopwatch, how the Digital Villages measured change over time and recorded their accomplishments from the starting line to the check-ered flag.

8 THE FINISH LINE:

MEASURING CHANGE OVER TIME

We have had a decent year, but we need that big finish to end the
year right. I am anxious for the first win. I am not obsessing about
it, but I am ready for it to happen so we can move on to the next
challenge.
—Vitor Meira

There are many ways to measure change over time. The focus may be on lap time or the finish line in a race. These correspond with program progress and outcomes. However, they all have one thing in common. They have at least two data points:[1] one before the intervention and another after the intervention.

We began this story with the ending—Digital Village success stories. These were really measurements of change over time. The Tribal Digital Village built the largest unlicensed[2] wireless system in the country and launched a successful digital printing press service. East Palo Alto Digital Village created an online resource center, digital community centers, and distributed hundreds of laptops to teachers and students. The Baltimore Digital Village distributed hundreds of computers and printers to families in their community and teachers in their schools. They also provided professional development training programs to local businesses. All of these accomplishments represent second data points, typically compared to a zero baseline when there was not any wireless system, digital printing service, or distribution of laptops to parents, teachers, and students.

There are many ways to document change over time. Everyone loves a story. Brief narratives[3] are an efficient way of documenting and highlighting outcomes. A few are included in this chapter. Photography[4] is an even more succinct manner of capturing and communicating about accomplishments. A picture is worth a thousand words, according to Barnard (1921). Illustrations, in the form of numbered figures, are sprinkled throughout this book. Storytelling[5] adds a more personal dimension to data collection. Photovoice[6] (photographs) and digital storytelling[7] (videocamera) were tools used to enable Digital Village members to tell their own story while highlighting program outcomes and impacts. They are useful approaches to accommodate diverse voices in a community.[8] The Digital Village empowerment evaluations relied on these among many other tools[9] to document successes and to identify areas meriting attention.

However, in telling their stories, the Digital Villages' most powerful language was the language of business: spreadsheets and bar charts.[10] This language was appropriate because most of the success stories were told by small business entrepreneurs to a donor—a big business—who also spoke their language.

TRIBAL DIGITAL VILLAGE

Contrary to popular belief, people do not overinflate ratings of their performance, particularly if they are committed to social change, personal growth, and community well-being. In fact, they are often hypercritical of their own performance because they want to do a better job and they want their programs to work. People working in less than optimal environments are often looking for a way to fix what's not working and to lead a more satisfying and productive life. Empowerment evaluation provides people with a window of opportunity to improve the organizational health of their work environments and to transform their communities' well-being.

The Tribal Digital Village is a good example of this honest, reflective, self-critical phenomenon. They made tremendous strides and accomplishments. However, like seasoned musicians assessing their own performance, they were harsh critics. They knew where their weaknesses were, what "notes" they missed, where they needed to improve, in spite of what a less well-trained eye might have judged as exceptional performance.

The Tribal Digital Village used the taking stock exercise to rate their individual activities. They used those ratings to come up with an overall average TDV rating (an average of the individual activity ratings). They began with a 5.2 on a 10-point scale—not an 8, 9, or 10. Nine months later they gave themselves an overall rating of 6.35. This is not the image of a self-congratulatory group. They did not assign themselves inflated scores or ratings. They considered their assessment to be realistic. Ratings for specific activities, such as building the network, were high because they built it. They were directly responsible for this accomplishment. They also rated equipment delivery highly, because delivery had significantly improved over time. However, they assigned credit where credit was due—to HP. Equipment delivery improved because HP routinized operations after the disruptive merger with Compaq. Improved HP delivery service meant in turn improved delivery service for the Digital Villages.

The Tribal Digital Village was also aware of its own Achilles' heel[11] and rated those activities accordingly. Governance, organizational structure, and management received low ratings. Ironically, they also rated themselves very conservatively when it came to funding. They were in a strong position to attain self-sufficiency, particularly in comparison with the other Digital Villages. They had built a wireless system, a digital printing press, and even attracted significant funds to their enterprise. However, they remained cautious and highly self-critical concerning their performance in vital areas like funding. To the untrained eye the low ratings seem too modest, self-critical, and possibly even inaccurate. They only measured and reported an increase of 1 point on a 10-point scale after all of their accomplishments. However, the insider's eye sees all. They were keenly aware of all the problems, missteps, and land mines in front of them (see Figures 11 and 12).

Narrative

The numbers rarely tell the whole story, and such is the case with the Tribal Digital Village. They had numerous stories to tell about how technology had an impact on the lives of people living on the reservation. Parents spoke about how their children were using the Internet to complete their homework, to conduct school research projects, and to learn about the world around them. There were many examples of unemployed members of the community using the Internet to search for and to secure employment.

The most powerful stories came from those who had successfully bridged the digital divide. They had made the crossover from no access to access. Jamul Indian Village tribal members, for example, did not have access to high-speed Internet services. The Tribal Digital Village's wireless system made this leap possible. One member of the community said, "It was like

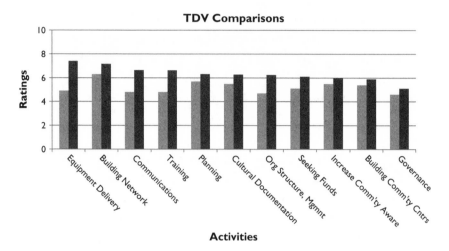

FIGURE 11. Tribal Digital Village's 1st and 2nd data point comparisons.

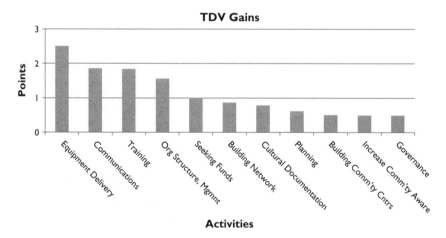

FIGURE 12. Tribal Digital Village's gains.

turning on a light bulb." The Internet lit the way out of the digital darkness for many of the tribes, ranging from access to educational opportunities to information about medical concerns. Jamal youth jumped at the opportunity to access the Web, ensuring a seamless transition from one generation to the next in the future.

EAST PALO ALTO DIGITAL VILLAGE

The East Palo Alto Digital Village's story was radically different from that of the Tribal Digital Village. They had not reached the goals they mapped out at the beginning of the project. In fact, they had fallen far short of those aspirations and were nearing the end of their funding. Their self-assessment was accurately characterized as modest at best.

The East Palo Alto Digital Village compared their original taking stock baseline self-assessment ratings with their second taking stock exercise ratings and reported a gain of less than 1 point (on the same 10-point scale). In some cases, such as management, their self-reported ratings went down. Fundraising was initially rated low and remained low (3 on a 10-point scale). This was a sobering comparison that placed their work in the harsh light of reality.

The data may not have been pretty, but the data stared them in the face. There was no place to turn, no place to hide. They had to look at the data. Instead of becoming demoralized and giving up, they reorganized, regrouped, and repackaged themselves. They chose to be constructive and to focus on their strengths instead of their weaknesses. They were not skilled at implementing and operating their own programs, but they were successful at helping others develop new programs. Similarly, they rated themselves poorly in terms of their own management skills, but they were skilled at providing management training for other small businesses in the community. They became known as a team of management consultants who helped start-up programs and provided training to support ongoing business ventures. They also knew how to integrate technology into people's daily lives. They built on these strengths and used them to buttress areas of perceived weakness (see Figures 13 and 14).

Narrative

The East Palo Alto Digital Village had an important story to tell. Their story had implications for each of the Digital Villages and for those engaged in comprehensive community initiatives in general. It was the story of a ripple in a pond. Every time the East Palo Alto Digital Village helped a business, a community agency, a teacher, a student, or a family member, they had an impact

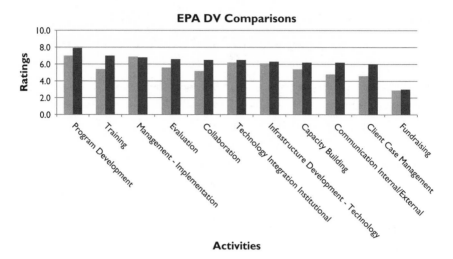

FIGURE 13. East Palo Alto Digital Village's 1st and 2nd data point comparisons.

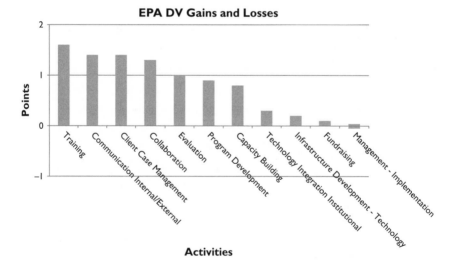

FIGURE 14. East Palo Alto Digital Village's gains and losses.

on another part of the community. This spoke in part to the tightly woven nature of the community. It also spoke to East Palo Alto Digital Village's relationship with the community. They were active members of the same community. They grew up in the same town. They worked there. They worshipped together. This relationship allowed for what one of the business marketing members of the team referred to as "deep penetration of the market."[12] In other words, they were a part of the social fabric of the community, which made their normal daily contacts resemble a strategic plan to leverage each and every contact. This multiplier effect made their efforts more efficient. It also speaks to the importance of having people initiate change in their own community. They had the credibility and the contacts, and they understood the context.

Refocusing their efforts and limiting their services to providing technical training and support for small businesses expanded their impact on the community exponentially. For example, one of their clients was a Montessori[13] childcare preschool. The director was a computer novice and requested basic computer skills training. Ostensibly the training was for her; however, she quickly applied what she had learned to the entire preschool. They had not used computers to operate the school before they received the training. These new skills enabled them to maintain and to access all their financial records, to communicate more effectively internally, and to issue monthly newsletters to their families. In addition to helping the school operate smoothly and efficiently, the use of computers freed up time for the director to focus on soliciting donations, recruiting new families, and monitoring her daycare providers. The mechanics were simple but the impact enormous. According to the director, "We learned how to make websites and how to use the Internet in our business. It (the training) literally doubled our numbers after putting what we learned to work." Moreover, she appreciated the power of the Internet to create webs of meaning within her own community. During one informal chat, a few months after training, she reflected on her new digital path, "I've found so many groups and things related to our work. The Internet connects you to your community."

The same story was told in many other settings throughout the community. The East Palo Alto Digital Village provided their local school with computer and Internet-based training. The principal used the training to improve management practices in the school. The teachers used it to communicate more effectively with parents. They also used it to revise their curriculum by requiring students to complete assignments online. This forced the students to access the Web on a routine basis. There was no alternative, so it became the norm. Students became web literate. They were also engaged. The Internet helped them learn to be highly motivated self-starters who could independently map out new educational terrain on their own.

The story did not end with the students. They brought their laptops home and taught their parents how to use their computers to search for jobs, to continue their education, and to identify resources in the community to improve their lives. The magnitude of the ripple effect was unanticipated but welcome. Success bred more success. Ironically the old tried-and-true method—word of mouth—was still one of the most effective means of spreading the high-tech word, that is, of helping to stimulate interest in and use of the Internet.

BALTIMORE DIGITAL VILLAGE

The Baltimore Digital Village's story is more about a successful turnaround than about a linear path toward success. They began with pride in their accomplishments, which included being selected by HP as a Digital Village. Pride was quickly transformed into organizational arrogance, manifested in part by their decision to uninvite their sponsor to a site visit. Although HP understood the circumstances and interpreted their behavior in the best possible light, the Digital Village may not have acted in their best interests. They missed a window of opportunity to help them learn how to communicate the same message in a much more diplomatic and constructive manner. It also emboldened them in such a way as to turn all manner of high-priced help and technical assistance away.

Once the Baltimore Digital Village ran the numbers and could see where they were when they started (rating themselves a 3 on a 10-point scale) and where they ended up (a 5 on a 10-point scale), they knew it was time to re-think their strategies. It was a rude but necessary awakening for their survival.

The first thing they did was to reopen communication with HP, who previously had offered their own internal expertise, external corporate consultants, technicians, and a host of other professionals. Most of the offers were either ignored or turned away. Now the Baltimore Digital Village was asking for help and listening to what talented individuals had to offer. They began by re-visiting the Deloitte & Touche report and then opened the door to others. They remained in the drivers seat by selecting the consultants they wanted to hear from and the tools they were going to use. However, they no longer turned away expertise without any thought or consideration again.

Second, they reassessed their organizational structure. They recognized why they never created a formal organizational entity to drive the Digital Village. It was because they did not have enough trust in the initiative to invest in it themselves. In addition, there was insufficient trust between the participating partners. This structural abnormality set them apart from the other Digital Villages. They realized this had to be remedied. The conversation shifted from promoting pet projects to focusing on projects valued across partners and for the common good of the community. They made formal agreements between the collaborating agencies with memoranda of agreement. This was a good start to turn things around. The conversation had evolved, and the Digital Village was ready to entertain the notion of creating a nonprofit umbrella operation to ensure institutional longevity. However, it remained at that level—a conversation entertaining the notion instead of an action step to create a more stable and enduring organizational structure.

The third major change was that they embraced evaluation on a day-to-day basis. Whereas the other Digital Villages were guided by empowerment evaluation and employed a host of traditional evaluation tools, the Baltimore Digital Village was slow to employ routine monitoring tools and devices to accompany their overall empowerment approach. After reviewing the data, they made a radical change in their behavior. They overcompensated in comparison to the other Digital Villages. They invited the empowerment evaluators to train each of the directors how to evaluate their own programs. They created baselines for everything under the sun. They spelled out the precise nature of the intervention, the program, or the strategy. The Baltimore Digital Village created benchmarks by specifying the numbers they wanted to reach and timelines to achieve them. According to an agreed-upon schedule, they compared their baseline and benchmarks with actual performance and accomplishments to determine if they were making progress. It was an evalu-

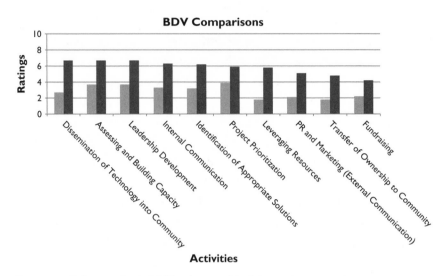

FIGURE 15. Baltimore Digital Village's 1st and 2nd data point comparisons.

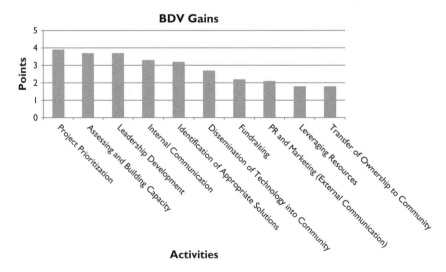

FIGURE 16. Baltimore Digital Village's gains.

ator's dream come true and it worked. They were still in control of the operation and evaluation. It was still an empowerment evaluation. However, it felt like an evaluation on steroids. The attention to detail, the follow-up, and way data were used to inform decision making made everyone stop and take notice. The entire process engendered trust and faith in the enterprise. It attracted volunteers, program participants, and funders. It also helped to place the entire operation back on track in the eleventh hour (see Figures 15 and 16).

Narrative

The Baltimore Digital Village had become mature enough to recognize the dysfunctional qualities they were exhibiting and to reflect on how their behavior was impacting their performance and potential. It took this kind of organizational crisis to enable them to see the educational and transformational[14] value of evaluation. In spite of their difficulties, the time required to turn things around, and how far they were from the finish line, they were making a contribution to the community.

They distributed laptops to approximately two hundred teachers in the Baltimore City Public School System. The Digital Village also encouraged the local school district to provide computer skills training for teachers to maximize the use of the laptops, specifically to help them improve their teaching. According to one teacher who participated in the training, "I've been able to access websites made especially for educators and through them find information that I would otherwise have no way to know about. I've used those sites to find lesson plans." She used the Internet to find new and exciting ways to engage her students in her class about the weather, including using animations, maps, and satellite images.

The Baltimore Digital Village's work in the school district also had a secondary and unanticipated impact. They convinced the district to evaluate the effectiveness of their training program. The data were used to improve the quality and effectiveness of the computer skills training program in the schools. The pretest and posttest[15] design caught the eye of one administrator after another. Program evaluation, which initially focused on professional development training, became a cultural norm or expectation in the school. After a handful of these trainings and corresponding evaluations were conducted in the school district, pretest and posttests could be found everywhere. In addition, professional development programs throughout the district that were unrelated to the Digital Village efforts started to employ the same basic pretest and posttest measures. The evaluation trend helped to improve program practice and accountability throughout the district.

The Baltimore Digital Village also made contributions to small businesses, improved residential access to the Internet, and created a useful web portal for the community. However, their success, like that of the other Digital Villages, goes far beyond the numbers. The neglected nano-stories of personal triumph are part of the larger, overall community success story.

It is hard for most people who grew up computer literate to imagine the layers of fear, doubt, and insecurity that accompany those left behind in the digital divide. Most of them blame themselves for not learning how to use the computer and the Internet. They do not realize they are part of a larger blaming the victim[16] game, a result of poor computer programming and poor instructional pedagogy. In many cases circumstances associated with socioeconomics, such as health, education, and employment, created a series of missed opportunities for them to learn. Building people's confidence enough to combat their fears, phobias, and perceived failures is an enormous task in and of itself. However, the Baltimore Digital Village's first order of business was to convince people to try and use computers and the Internet, particularly if it was their first time. They also charged themselves with the responsibility of convincing members of their community to try again, if they had not succeeded in the past. For example, Shauna, a teaching assistant, received basic computer training and it changed her life. "At first, I was really intimidated by using a computer, but the classes really helped me get over that." Shauna started using the Internet to develop lesson plans and communicate with parents. It gave her the confidence to further her own education and to significantly enhance her life options.

The Baltimore Digital Village excelled at precisely this task—the personal level—the first building block in community capacity building. Much like the other Digital Villages, the Baltimore Digital Village's success in this area was in large part due to their close personal ties, contacts, and relationships in the community.

CONCLUSION

Spreadsheets and bar charts, narratives, and photography all tell a part of the Digital Village story. However, these highly self-critical stories only scratch the surface. The story told thus far would commit a sin of omission if it did not bring to the surface the underlying or hidden curriculum: building capacity. The heart of the Digital Village story is what was left behind—the capacity of these communities to continue to grow and to prosper on their own. The next chapter highlights the role of capacity building, the training tracks that made members of the Digital Village the real winners in this race to bridge the digital divide.

9 THE REAL WINNERS:

BUILDING CAPACITY

> To finish first you must first finish.
> —Rick Mears

There is more to this story. Most of the story thus far has focused on processes,[1] outcomes,[2] and accomplishments. However, the hidden story is about capacity building, which is about people learning new skills and competencies in order to more effectively manage their own affairs.[3] Most of capacity building happens in the background; it is what happens along the way. However, cultivating capacity is no accident. It must be a planned and purposeful process that operates on multiple levels.

Capacity building requires repetition. It is a habit of the mind that shapes and guides thought and behavior. Capacity building is composed of hundreds of interconnected and reinforcing behaviors each and every day. They range from shadowing a mentor[4] to learn about their routine to a simple wink of approval. Over the course of a year, they impact hundreds of decisions and millions of synaptic connections and chemical reactions in our brains. Although it is ongoing and multifaceted, for those facilitating capacity building, it is the culmination of a way of seeing the world and a way of treating people. It is a hand up, not a handout, approach. For those building their own capacity, it requires an attitude toward life that embraces opportunities, learns from them, and builds on both knowledge and experience.

One thread running through the social fabric of Digital Village capacity building was the training ground phenomenon. The training ground is a place where people learn how to do something new. It may be a carpenter apprentice learning the trade or a medical student learning to be doctor. It is an opportunity to occupy a role that allows for on-the-job training. On every level, members of the Digital Villages were provided with opportunities to occupy roles they would otherwise not have been considered for or would have been formally denied. This opportunity allowed them to operate in what Vygotsky (1978) called the proximal zone.[5] It is a place just beyond a person's reach and experience. It is somewhere between what a person can do on their own without help and what they can do with the assistance of a more experienced individual. It places them outside their comfort zone. The proximal zone is where people learn to stretch themselves and reach another level of insight, understanding, and capacity. In this case, members of the Digital Village occupied a physical role in the real world that placed them squarely in the proximal zone as planners, designers, managers, employers, and employees in training.

A few brief Digital Village vignettes are presented, highlighting the role of the training ground phenomenon in capacity building. It was a multi-level, transparent, formal and informal, but intentional, process of building capacity. The following section provides insight into the silent building blocks of the Digital Village that contributed to self-efficacy and to sustainability.

HEWLETT-PACKARD

Capacity building is at the heart of the Digital Village dream. It begins with the desire to help people help themselves. One of the objectives of capacity building is for people to take control over their own lives. Successful capacity building, for the group cultivating capacity building, requires a willingness to let go of the reigns of power and the need to be in control all the time. HP started and ended with this underlying philosophy and orientation for the Digital Village. HP was a corporate and a philanthropic model of capacity building. They helped three diverse minority communities to define their own community-based mission, to build their own entrepreneurial bridges across the digital divide, and to learn from both their successes and missteps. They did not simply hand over the money and walk away from the Digital Village communities. That would have been an abdication of their responsibility. They selected the communities and wanted them to succeed. They made an investment in them by providing the tools required to build capacity, ranging from financial resources to technical assistance and expertise. They also provided them with the essential non-tangibles, the trust and freedom to embark on a journey of this magnitude. It was a journey toward self-sufficiency and sustainability.

HP's training ground was Digital Village senior management. It provided Digital Village leaders with the opportunity to govern and to manage operations. Digital Village executive directors managed the entire enterprise. They had to handle finance, policy, human relations, facilities, public relations, and a host of critical organizational concerns. They planned projects, supervised employees, and built businesses. Digital Village leaders were able to jump to the front of the management lines and the top of the pyramid of power, in the same manner that they helped community members leapfrog across the digital divide. Instead of waiting a lifetime for an opportunity to run a business of this scale, they were given the opportunity immediately and they seized it. They learned what it took to run a complex organization by doing it. There is a place for studying management, but it is difficult to compete with this kind of guided experiential learning.[6]

One of the Digital Village executive directors faced a steep learning curve in his role. He had a handful of personnel issues to confront, ranging from hiring to firing. He had not learned to delegate these responsibilities at this point in his tenure. He described what his experience was like in this role at that time, "There are times when I feel absolutely overwhelmed and then the next day after a talk with one of the HP folks it makes sense. Some of it is just common sense, but with a lot of legalize and bureaucratize. The bottom line is that I have to learn how to just hand some of it off, but it is still on my head." He was learning how to manage from a senior level, allowing HR to handle what they knew best. At the same time, he realized "the buck stops here." Ultimately, the decisions made by his team on his watch as stewards of the organization were his responsibility. This was a typical senior management learning scenario across Digital Villages. Executive directors dove into the role, managed the role (and the Digital Villages) based on varied business and management experience, received varying degrees of mentorship and assistance, and muddled through. It was not always a clean, academically precise learning or doing—but it worked.

HP was not naïve. They anticipated problems and recognized that the Digital Villages would need assistance—thus the bank of consultants and management mentors HP made available to the Digital Village leadership. HP helped them succeed and also allowed them to fail (with a safety net). In addition to learning their roles along the way, senior management gained experience that placed them one major step ahead of the game when it came time to compete for similar leadership positions outside the Digital Village in the future.

THE DIGITAL VILLAGES

The Digital Villages supported the development of small businesses, schools, and nonprofits in their communities. They provided them with the equipment, talent, training, and related resources to accomplish their economic and educational objectives. They expected small businesses, schools, and nonprofits to remain in control of their organizations. They were expected to determine precisely what they wanted to do and how they wanted to do it. The small community businesses were in charge of implementing their own dream. Once again the combination of freedom and support, which HP had modeled, became the backbone of the Digital Village framework. It worked because it was not a disconnected patchwork. It was a way of life. Organizationally, this philosophy was embedded within their normal operating procedures.

The Digital Village training ground was most visible on the project level. Digital Village leadership gave Digital Village managers and local community members ample opportunity to design and to implement their own projects. Their proposals were evaluated in much the same way proposals are submitted and reviewed for consideration in other walks of life. However, the project managers typically were individuals who had never occupied roles of this nature before, assumed this level of responsibility, or commanded this level of respect.

The Digital Village project managers took the reigns and rode with them. They had to plan and to schedule tasks, to hire people, to monitor progress, to provide feedback and assistance, and to produce on time. These are important and transferable skills and competencies.[7] One Digital Village manager who was having problems rolling out his program of delivering laptops to the local schools described his experience,

> This is a big headache. The laptops are just sitting in boxes on pallets in a warehouse. It has been months. They are on my back [the executive director and senior

leaders in his Digital Village]. They have to report to HP that we haven't even delivered the computers they gave us, but they don't understand it is not that simple. We have to tag them and go through all the requests and then hire folks to distribute them. You can't just hand them out. But I was talking with my pastor and he showed me what they do during Thanksgiving when they give away the groceries to those who need help and it all started to fall in place. I shared this with my director and he explained the idea of a supply chain[8] that he heard from a talk he went to [parenthetically which was supplied by HP] and it all really fell into place.

This manager had some experience in this area but certainly not at this level and with this much exposure—if it went wrong (which it did) he faced community criticism, senior management rebukes, and a perceived HP pressure. He was, however, resourceful. He went to sources he trusted including his pastor, which gave him both the practical techniques and the moral authority, as it were, to continue (in spite of his lack of success in the area). In addition, he was working in an organizational context that helped guide the way—directly from his manager and indirectly from the training and information provided by HP to his senior manager. It was an indirect and informal path, but once again it was the immersion in the job and in a supportive (and informed) community that helped him accomplish his objectives and crystallize the learning experience for the future.

Motivation was another critical capacity-building variable in this human equation. The project managers were personally committed to the project and valued the opportunity and trust they were given to operate these programs. They also had a stake in the community because they were members of the community. They returned to their communities each night, so there was no place to hide. Just as the Digital Village leadership team was advantaged by this opportunity, project managers had a leg up in any comparable competition concerning employment opportunities given their experience.

EMPOWERMENT EVALUATION

Capacity building is one of the ten principles guiding empowerment evaluation.[9] It is such an important principle that if there is no capacity building present in a project, then it is probably not an empowerment evaluation. Clearly, the selection of empowerment evaluation to guide this initiative was no random accident. Empowerment evaluation was selected because it was philosophically and practically in alignment with the Digital Village's commitment to capacity building and program improvement.

There is no waiting period, delay, or probationary period in an empowerment evaluation. Empowerment evaluations begin with the community in control, and just as HP immediately handed over control to the Digital Village leadership, the Digital Village leadership handed over control to local community-based businesses and nonprofits.

The training ground in an empowerment evaluation is the evaluation (see Figure 17). Instead of training to conduct an evaluation, Digital Village leadership, management, and community members simply conducted their own evaluation (with the assistance of a critical friend/evaluation coach). Conducting the evaluation was the training.[10] They learned by doing (Dewey, 2009; Lewin, 1948). The immediacy of the experience propelled people into action. It also created a sense of ownership, which enhanced commitment and follow-through.

Typically I would facilitate the initial or introductory exercises. However, I would conduct it with a member of the Digital Village or community member who had an interest in (and in one case some experience conducting) an evaluation. Quickly I transferred the responsibility to that person (with me as a support person as needed). For example, in the Tribal Digital Village, I facilitated the first exercise with Dr. Linda Locklear, one of the tribal members in the Digital Village. During the second exercise I reversed the roles. Linda was in charge and I served as a support person. She was ready for it. Linda was used to crossing tribal lines. She was a boundary spanner (Daft, 1989). She was used to straddling the needs of social service agencies (and now the Digital Village) with the needs of individual tribes. She said, "They all know me. I have relatives in that tribe too [a tribe other than her own]. I am always knocking on doors to get things done."

I would still help her prepare for sessions and debrief her after them to learn from each experience. We maintained this partnership throughout the evaluation. However, she was the face of the evaluation for the Tribal Digital Village, not me. People learned to look to her instead of me during meetings and exercises. Most of the time this worked. Once in a while I was asked to

FIGURE 17. East Palo Alto Digital Village member taking stock by entering her ratings on poster paper using 1 (low) to 10 (high) point scale.

step in or we brought in another tribal member because of some baggage or past experience that got in the way. The same approach was applied to the other Digital Villages. This transition and substitution technique, working myself out of a job, is an integral part of building capacity.

The same approach applied to using methods, including sorting data in spreadsheets, digital photography,[11] videoconferencing,[12] and online surveys.[13] Members of the Digital Village added their collective thoughts to the formulation of a mission statement, used dots to set priorities for tasks, entered the taking stock ratings into an Excel spreadsheet, tabulated the results, and displayed the ratings by projecting the results on an LCD (liquid crystal display) projector with the group. They also documented each activity with digital photography and used their pictures to tell their story. They observed critical activities, such as building a tower or computer skills training sessions, and documented them. They also conducted pre- and post-online surveys to assess community response to Digital Village interventions. They learned to think like an evaluator by conducting the evaluation themselves (Fetterman, 2012a).

The skeptic might ask, How is this possible? People often ask the same question during my workshops.[14] They say, "evaluation is too complex to be handed off to amateurs." In response I ask one of them to take my camera and take a picture of me while I highlight an important point about people's native capacity to collect data and to evaluate in my presentation. The audience laughs as the participant snaps a photograph of me making such a serious point. I stop the demonstration and rhetorically ask, "What did I just do?"—aside from sharing a vain moment with them? My answer, "I just transferred a skill of evaluation, silently, transparently, and powerfully. That participant just helped us record part of the workshop—photographically." That is how simple and transparent the process can and should be.

The same well-thought-out but transparent approach applied to helping HP leadership and managers as applied to helping staff and community members as they established baselines, goals, and benchmarks to evaluate their programs. Whether it is evaluation design, method, or management, people from all walks of life are capable of learning how to evaluate their own programs. There is no substitution for learning by doing in a psychologically "safe environment" guided by seasoned coaches, facilitators, and mentors.

CONCLUSION

The same principles of capacity building applied to the entire Digital Village experience, including HP, Digital Village leadership, staff, community members, and empowerment evaluators. HP handed over the reigns to Digital Village leadership. Digital Village leaders and managers learned by being immersed in the Digital Village experience but with guidance. The entire process was transparent as people filled roles that allowed them to learn from doing. The same held true in the community for small business people, nonprofit staff members, and families in the community. They learned to use hardware, software, and the Internet in new ways, expanding their view of what could be done to grow and to expand their operations. Small businesses learned how to broaden their markets, to focus their marketing campaigns, to maximize profits, and generally to enhance their businesses. One local business person set up a webpage with a host of cleaning tips to attract more customers to his cleaning service. Another was thrilled to learn how to use a database,

> With these lists (of suppliers and customers) all in one place I don't have to go running around any more to track someone down when I need to place an order or service my machinery. I am learning to spend less on advertising by making a list of my most loyal customers. They showed me how to sort the "data base" to find them. The hardest part was putting their names and addresses in but once it's in I

just push these buttons. I can see who shops here the most. I can even see what they bought. I am sending fliers just to them, my loyal customers, this week.

They learned all of these strategies from the Digital Village trainers and facilitators. This experiential approach toward capacity building (on all levels) is an art form when conducted with sensitivity, finesse, and experience.

In race car driving school, as discussed earlier, you learn to race at 70 to 80 percent of your capacity. Why? Because if you are driving at full capacity all the time you are just hanging on for dear life, surviving each corner. You can not learn anything new that way. When you drive below your capacity you can hear, absorb, and learn from your driving coach. Part of capacity building is learning by doing. Speed, like time, is of the essence. There is no time to lose or another generation will be left behind in the digital age. However, capacity building, similar to the education of a medical student in a teaching hospital, needs extra time built into the fast-paced process to learn and to absorb the experience and instruction. The concluding chapter is reflexive. It represents time that has been built into this journey to reflect and to synthesize what's been learned on the track today.

10 REFLECTIONS ON THE RACE TOWARD SOCIAL JUSTICE: WHAT HAVE WE LEARNED?

Success is where preparation and opportunity meet.
—Bobby Unser

The first thing we learned is that placing the community in charge of its future works. In a comprehensive community initiative of this magnitude and design, self-empowerment pays off. It produces real-world, credible outcomes. The Tribal Digital Village built the largest unlicensed wireless system in the country and a digital printing press company. The East Palo Alto and Baltimore Digital Villages distributed hundreds of laptops to students and their teachers and in the process influenced teaching and school district curriculum. Small businesses around the country flourished as a result of Digital Village training and expertise. These are significant community returns on investment (CROI),[1] demonstrating that people can make a difference in their own communities.

We also learned that you can create community among diverse groups. In the East Palo Alto Digital Village, African Americans, Latinos, and Pacific Islanders often battled with each other over scarce resources.[2] Similarly, in the Tribal Digital Village warring tribal factions viewed the simplest misunderstandings through a lens of age-old disputes.[3] The Baltimore Digital Village consisted of a collection of small businesses and nonprofits with a history of competition instead of cooperation. However, in each of these cases, the groups came together based on common interests. The unity was not a function of a utopian[4] ideal of brother or sisterhood. It was based on shared common interests—or more precisely vested interests.[5] If a group decided not to participate, their voice would not be heard and their interests would not be represented. People felt compelled to attend and to participate if they wanted their seat at the table, if they wanted to influence or shape the conversation about change in their communities. The convergence of vested interests created a common social denominator.

The power of this group process—a community building process—still depended on the strength of each individual. People took responsibility for making change happen in their lives. No one empowered anyone, people empowered themselves. People were their own advocate and their own change agent in order to effect community-based change.

Systemic, comprehensive, large-scale changes in a community rest on the shoulders of these individually empowered human beings. However, no one can make these kinds of changes all by themselves. Systemic change requires a partnership. Anything worthwhile, such as bringing an enterprise to scale in order to bridge the digital divide, requires teamwork. The Digital Village partnership relied on a tried-and-true triumvirate: corporate philanthropy (HP), academe (Stanford University), and the community (three minority communities of color located across the country). This team helped to build the road to the Digital Village's success while driving on it.

An effort of this scope also requires management skills and group planning. "Managing a community change effort requires maintaining a complex web of relationships among residents, funders, intermediaries, neighborhood organizations, public sector agencies, private sector financial institutions, and consultants" (Kubisch et al., 2010, p. ix). Group plans must be rooted in community concerns. They also need to be developed within the context of what people are already being held accountable for in their program or community. This makes it credible and ensures that individual efforts remain in alignment with the larger goals and outcomes of the community. It also ensures an additional measure of accountability.

We also learned that capacity building was the key to sustainability.[6] Capacity building and mentorship were integral parts of the Digital Village plan, at every stage and at every level. Capacity building was part of the hidden curriculum. Digital Village directors and managers learned how to operate their Digital Village by being given the opportunity to "run the business." They did, however, receive HP supported training, advice, and mentorship. Young adults learned how to repair the routers for the Tribal Digital Village, but not without assistance. Cisco experts provided the training.

Similarly, Digital Village members learned how to use evaluation to monitor, to assess, and to improve their own performance. They learned how to think like an evaluator and conduct an evaluation by doing it themselves. The Digital Villages remained in control of their evaluation. However, they did not do it alone. They were guided by empowerment evaluators. This learning by doing model created an ownership of the learning process. As Kubisch et al. (2010, pp. ix–x) explain,

> Evaluation in community change work has been increasingly viewed as a means to enhance real-time learning and decision-making, refine strategy, and institute midcourse corrections. Soliciting the opinions and priorities of multiple and diverse stakeholders in developing key evaluation questions cultivates ownership of the learning process and increases the likelihood that results will be useful, relevant, and credible for potential users. The iterative process of learning and doing helps to position evaluation as a tool for improving practices and nurturing change at every level. No longer an outsourced function, it becomes the collective responsibility of all stakeholders. In order to support this process, funders and evaluators must often work hard to provide sufficient resources and structures to support learning, and to create a culture that values candid dialogue and analysis and embraces the idea of learning while doing.

Members of the Digital Village learned by doing, but no one abdicated their responsibility. Everyone stayed in the game to monitor, to mentor, and to assist. This type of support created a virtual "safety net" and training ground. In addition, the high degree of community participation and control cultivated a sense of ownership. Community ownership, in turn, contributed to commitment. The community took responsibility for the long-term success of the project.

The Digital Village was a shining example of how a hand up contributes to self-determination[7] (in contrast to the maladaptive model of a hand out, which has fostered dependency[8] in the past). The training ground model generated a sense of responsibility, commitment, and capacity that extended far beyond the Digital Village. They learned how to establish a focus or purpose, to set priorities, to assess, to create agendas, to use data to inform decision making, to listen to their communities, and to access additional resources. This kind of capacity building was designed to enhance sustainability. This practice-based insight parallels Kubisch et al.'s (2010, p. ix) findings:

> For broad community change efforts, these investments must move beyond build-ing the capacity to implement a particular initiative and instead focus on building the capacity of a community to set agendas, gain access to resources, and respond to community needs.

Digital Village members took what they learned with them and applied it to new frontiers within the Digital Village and outside of the walls of the village.

CHALLENGES

The long list of impressive outcomes is not to suggest that it was smooth sail-ing throughout the effort or that mistakes or missteps were not made. There were plenty of errors and lessons learned along the way. One of the Digital Village directors reflected on one of the more trying days, "If they say we learn more from our mistakes than we do from our successes, then we must be bril-liant by now." The experience was both exhilarating and exhausting. It was humbling for even the most experienced players in the game. In the spirit of honesty, candor, and transparency, a few of the more problematic lessons learned are shared to help complete the Digital Village story. They are stories told in retrospect, about things that could not be seen at the time, but which with time and distance have become apparent. These lessons focus on areas for improvement.

Hewlett-Packard

HP could have done more to facilitate communication between the Digital Villages from the onset of the project. Routine conference calls could have been scheduled for the directors. Periodic meetings and conferences, much like cluster evaluations,[9] could have been organized, in which representa-tives from each level share with their peers what worked, what they needed help with, and what was not working. A few attempts were made to connect the Digital Villages, but there was no ongoing dialogue or conversation between them. The few times the Digital Villages came into contact, such as when they were investigating the equipment delivery delays across the villages, the learning was multi-level, multi-purpose, and multi-dimensional. It was explosive and cathartic. Additional communication could have saved the following:

- Energy—sharing things that worked with each other to reduce the energy and resources associated with re-inventing the wheel
- Time—sharing lessons learned to prevent each of the Digital Villages from wasting time making many of the same missteps
- Money—sharing information about qualified and reasonably priced vendors and suppliers because they were involved in many of the same types of activities

Out of respect for self-governance, HP did not force its long list of consultants and technical experts on the Digital Villages. This is commendable. However, there were many occasions in which the Digital Villages might have benefited from HP-supported expertise at a much earlier stage in their development. In the one instance in which HP "pushed" the advice of experts on a Digital Village, it backfired. It was not offered, it was imposed. In addition, it was not conducted or delivered on the Digital Village's own terms. Moreover, it was not aimed at their stage of development or in a language they could understand at the time. HP might have considered requiring the Digital Villages to listen—not to follow but to listen—to the advice of experts at predictable pivotal points and at appropriate stages of development.

People need to be held accountable, even in the most altruistic and humanitarian endeavors. HP required reports and periodic updates. However, they did not tie compensation or payment to achievement or time on task, as they do in their own business. Securing full funding made some Digital Villages too comfortable. It gave them a false sense of security and allowed them to think they had all the time in the world. It also allowed them to divert their attention and focus to other opportunities since this one was in hand. This pushed the Digital Villages into the catch-up game and left them scurrying around at the end of each year to accomplish agreed upon goals. When the Digital Villages worked well, they accomplished a great deal with quality.

However, when they were rushed and racing to meet unrealistic deadlines, quality often suffered.

HP realized that the next time around it might be wise to help them develop shorter timelines with clearly stated intermediate goals to track progress more effectively and keep everyone on task. In addition, payments could be tied to quarterly accomplishments and goals. This suggestion is more complex than it might appear because everyone was in a discovery mode, learning while doing. In some cases, the time to complete a task was more a random guess than a calculated and well-thought-out estimate. However, this approach toward increased monitoring and accountability would have required Digital Villages to be sufficiently aware of operations to be able to provide legitimate explanations for delays or detours.

Digital Villages

Instead of viewing the enterprise as a friendly competition, the Digital Villages could have embraced the concept of cooperation from day one. Competition made much of the learning redundant and inefficient. Although each Digital Village had to learn its own lessons, there were many mechanical lessons that did not bear repeating and could have saved both time and money.

In addition, this competitive spirit made the Digital Villages "grow up" in silos instead of a much richer environment of shared experience and expertise. HP contributed to this isolation; they valued the competitive spirit and did not want the villages to excessively influence one another. However, the Digital Villages could have taken the initiative to turn this type of communication (or lack thereof) around and to create an even larger and more dynamic "liquid network" in which good ideas flow like water down a stream.

Similarly, one of the Digital Villages could have taken the initiative and embraced the expertise offered much sooner in their own development and benefited from it. However, for them exhilaration quickly became transformed into hubris, which proved to be self-defeating.

Empowerment Evaluation

Empowerment evaluation could have been a better mirror, to help the less secure Digital Village see their performance at an earlier stage in their development. Confident Digital Villages understood the approach and consumed it immediately. The less confident or more conflict-ridden Digital Village could not see the value as quickly and, like HP, the empowerment evaluators were almost too respectful of their boundaries. Instead of waiting for the invitation as recommended, the empowerment evaluators could have been more aggressive about the need to establish baselines, goals, and benchmarks much sooner. In addition, the empowerment evaluators could have been more confident about "speaking their truth" when it came to potentially dysfunctional behavior, such as uninviting the sponsor to a site visit. Adopting a respectful, but more coach-like, posture might have helped one of the Digital Villages remain on task and on target much sooner.

The empowerment evaluators might have spotted some maladaptive group dynamics sooner, including individual power plays and manipulative behavior. For example, some members of the Digital Village would use "PC talk," or politically correct speech,[10] to divert or to control the conversation. Others repeatedly referred to "process" as a way of highjacking the dialogue. Legitimate PC moments and questions about process were appropriate. However, it was the manipulative use of these tools to control the group, to place themselves at the center, and to temporarily derail working groups that might have been recognized sooner rather than later.

The empowerment evaluators were reminded of the value of inclusion when they were asked not to invite specific individuals at each Digital Village because they were too negative, nasty, or not productive. However, in each case their presence proved to be invaluable. Although they were often prone to exaggeration and extreme in their views, their participation had the effect of emboldening other members of the Digital Village to speak about their concerns, which appeared pale by comparison. (However, previous to hearing these vocal members comment on the status of the program, participants thought their issues were potentially too negative, divisive, and delicate to mention.)

Overall Challenge

The overall challenge for comprehensive community change initiatives is to learn from both our successes and our missteps. The challenge is summarized by Kubisch et al. (2010, p. ix),

The challenge, then, is to apply what we have learned about the importance of a clear mission, good management, effective partnerships, and results accountability within the more fluid ecology of a distressed neighborhood located in a porous region. We need new ways of being strategic when we are working in a complex adaptive system. We need new ways of managing the work when we have to interact with so many actors. We need new forms of accountability when we are innovating and trying unproven strategies. We need new ways of defining success when we control so little. We need new ways of learning when causal connections are diffuse and difficult to establish. This is the charge to the next generation of community change work.

CONCLUSION

Digital Village learning was ongoing and periodically exponentially explosive. It was learning by doing. Digital Village members found this experiential approach to education intellectually and emotionally intoxicating. For many it felt like my son learning to sing his "do re mi" scales for the first time. His eyes lit up and his grin was from ear to ear. He was so proud of himself. Almost everyone associated with the development of the Digital Villages experienced this same type of uninhibited, almost childlike, expression of pride and accomplishment.

Empowerment evaluation taught people to see curves in the road of program implementation as opportunities. As people learned how to apply the breaks at the right time in order to negotiate the turn, they also positioned themselves in a manner that maximized their exit speed. This enabled them to return to their work prepared to better serve their communities without delay or detour. The empowerment evaluation approach was similar to teaching a person to drive, except the coaches were trained to race and the car was fueled with a desire as powerful as nitromethane in the gas tank. Some people may not care about speed, but on the road toward social justice, justice delayed is justice denied. The Digital Village was part of a much larger race toward social justice, and speed mattered.

DRIVING DOWN THE ROAD TOWARD SOCIAL JUSTICE
USING AN EMPOWERMENT EVALUATION ENGINE

A few driving tips that emerged from this drive down the road toward social justice include maximizing road surface to improve efficiency, aiming for the apex to maximize entry and exit time, and breaking to speed up.

Maximizing Road Surface. Empowerment evaluation helped members of the Digital Villages maximize their time by showing them how to drive on the entire road. If you imagine a serpentine path with one curve to the right followed by a curve to the left, and then back again to the right, you can also see a straight line that cuts across all of the snake-like curves. Instead of steering the car to make the wheels match the contours of every corner, you drive right through the centerline. That is the driver's line—the straightest path possible on the track—turning curves into straight lines.[11]

Empowerment evaluation helped Digital Village communities see and drive the straightest possible path to their destination. Empowerment evaluators helped members of the Digital Village to zero in on the most critical aspects of their operation, to identify specific strengths and weaknesses, and to use that data to design meaningful interventions that improved performance and helped make people's dreams come true. The empowerment evaluation approach saved time, money, and a very precious resource—human energy.

Aiming for the Apex. Curves are viewed as opportunities, not as obstacles or crises in empowerment evaluations. It is not the angle of the curve that matters. It is the way one confronts and negotiates it that matters. Empowerment evaluators helped members of the Digital Villages learn how to aim for the programmatic apex, the center of the organizational turn that produces the safest and fastest entry and exit speed, and thus placed them back on their programmatic track.

This was accomplished in part by helping people to say where they were going—their mission. A group can move more quickly once they have an agreed upon destination in common. In addition, empower-ment evaluators helped Digital Village community members steer to-ward the most efficient path by helping them to list their priorities for activities to be evaluated because they did not have the time or desire to evaluate everything. The evidence used to support a view or position during the taking stock step was leveraged to also serve as an indicator and evidence of performance in planning for the future interventions. These three steps, establishing a mission, taking stock, and planning for the future, were the primary apexes of this empowerment evalua-tion. They were all geared toward helping people learn to drive more effectively.

Braking. Empowerment evaluators taught members of the Digital Village how to apply the brakes in a way that helped them to speed up as they exited the challenging road conditions of organizational and community life. Empowerment evaluation helped them become more decisive and less timid as they encountered problems. Empowerment evaluators encouraged members of the Digital Village to keep moving fast and forward, avoiding indecision, delay, and doubt. Empowerment evaluators do not encourage people to throw caution to the wind. To the contrary, all safety measures were required. Educated guesses and data-base decision making—not random leaps of faith—were encouraged. Just as a safety belt and a helmet are required in racing, prudent judg-ment, evidence-based decision making, and financial responsibility were considered minimum mandates in this group decision-making experi-ence. Once the turn is negotiated, however, the programs were back on track in a manner that helped them accelerate their operations and better serve their communities.

Each of these driving tips helped members of the Digital Villages to see around the curves in the road, that is, to anticipate and to embrace problems. It was around the corners that real learning took place, and it was powered by an empowerment evaluation engine on the road toward social justice.

SOCIAL JUSTICE AND EVALUATION

My own work in empowerment evaluation has been accurately categorized as emancipatory[12] in nature because it helps people to help themselves and to become more self-determined. The primary purpose of the Digital Village was to ensure that people were not left behind in the digital divide. This is particularly important in the Digital Village communities, because the people left behind were disproportionately of color. In addition, the Digital Village empowerment evaluation was designed to ensure that members of the Digital Village remained in control of the enterprise and directly benefited from the data (to help inform their decision making).

This combination of evaluation and social justice is not new. They have a long history of working together hand-in-hand. MacDonald (1976) and House (1980) helped to bring the relationship to the surface decades ago. They explained how evaluation questions frequently reflect the concerns of a particular interest group. Even the choice of methods used in an evaluation reflect assumptions about who has access to the information and who is it designed to serve. More recently, Kirkhart (2010) contributed to the dialogue by examining evaluation theory in a cultural context, in which she focused on multicultural validity. Klugman (2010) highlighted values[13] associated with social justice pursuits and emphasized the role of evaluation in strengthening organizational capacity. Klugman's work has implications for what you evaluate, how you evaluate, and who evaluates.

Whitmore et al. (2006) used (1) empowerment evaluation, (2) the monitoring of "most significant changes," and (3) transformative evaluation approaches to illustrate what evaluation looks like when it endeavors to "achieve the goals of program improvement, understanding lived experience, and social justice."

My generation of evaluators have been influenced by our own personal commitment to civil rights. We remember learning about *Brown v. Board of Education*[14] and the Supreme Court's decision of 1954 that outlawed segregation in the public schools, the Civil Rights Bill,[15] and hearing the stirring words of Dr. Martin Luther King concluding his "I Have a Dream"[16] speech (1963): "Free at last! Free at last! Thank God Almighty, we are free at last." The Digital Village story is a part of this stream of civil rights and social justice in American history. It also demonstrates how evaluation can contribute to the pursuit of social justice.

ENGAGING IN A PUBLIC DIALOGUE

The Digital Village work was valued and prized internally. However, they also received accolades from high-ranking outside observers, ranging from the former head of the Federal Communications Commission to the president of the United States. The Rev. Jesse L. Jackson Sr. commented that the "initiative is fulfilling the mission of transforming the digital divide into digital opportunities for schools and students, businesses and communities." The HP chairman and chief executive officer during the initiative, Carly Fiorina, also publically recognized their efforts, "The progress you've made is homegrown, bottom-up, grass-roots. We may have added fuel to the dream, but the dream started with you."

As in the steps of empowerment evaluation, it is not enough to simply evaluate. The question is, What's next? The next steps might include replication or adaptation[17] of the Digital Village to an even larger scale proposition. The success of the Digital Villages has helped to open the door of opportunity for others to enter and to engage in this same type of community capacity building.

Their success has also created a window of opportunity—a space—to engage a broader public dialogue. The question is, If we know how to successfully engage in large-scale community change initiatives, what do we want our nation to look like in the future? We have models to work with, including the Digital Village triumvirate. By their very existence, these examples stimulate the imagination, generate a sense of excitement about the future, and leverage resources. "The presence of an organized, legitimate, and effective community intervention in a neighborhood increases its visibility and influence, helping to leverage new public, private, and philanthropic resources" (Kubisch et al., 2010, p. 44).

Although the Digital Village is a successful model, it is far from being the only one operating in the public arena. The Sustainable Communities program, launched by the Local Initiatives Support Corporation, is working in over sixty communities throughout the United States (Weissbourd, 2010).

Another successful collaborative in the health domain is the Community-Campus Partnerships for Health.[18] They are a network of over two thousand communities and campuses across North America that collaborate for the following purposes:

> to promote health through service-learning, community-based participatory research,[19] broad-based coalitions and other partnership strategies. These partnerships are powerful tools for improving higher education, civic engagement and the overall health of communities.

Government agencies, including the Environmental Protection Agency[20] and the Centers for Disease Control and Prevention, are committed to community-based strategies, actively engaging the community and inviting them to participate more fully in identifying and solving its own problems. The Obama administration is focusing neighborhood initiatives to support community-based initiatives. For example, the Neighborhood Revitalization Initiative is an interagency collaborative moving in this direction. It is led by the White House Domestic Policy Council and Office of Urban Affairs and the Departments of Housing and Urban Development, Education, Justice, Health and Human Services, and Treasury. The Institute for Translational Science (funded by the National Institutes of Health) promotes research conducted by tribal communities,[21] with the aim of involving communities in every stage of health research and to promote studies that address their priorities and health concerns.

The list of foundations committed to comprehensive community-based initiatives read like a veritable "who's who" in philanthropy. For example, the Kellogg Foundation[22] and the Marin Community Foundation have used empowerment evaluation. The Annie E. Casey Foundation adopted a similar approach[23] when they evaluated Making Connections, a comprehensive community initiative in ten urban neighborhoods across the United States. It also informed their work on the Community Health Worker Evaluation Toolkit. The MacArthur Foundation generously supports similar Sustainable Communities efforts. An abbreviated list of foundations[24] and their comprehensive community initiatives is provided in Table 1 to illustrate the scope of this national movement toward community collaboration, improvement, and empowerment.

TABLE 1
Organizations Using Empowerment Evaluation

American Legacy Foundation	Tobacco Use Cessation and Prevention
Mary Black Foundation	The Healthy Community Initiative
The California Endowment	The Public Health Initiative's Partnership for the Public's Health Rural Community Assistance Corporation's Agriculture Worker Health and Housing Program
The California Wellness Foundation	The Health Improvement Initiative The Children and Youth Community Health Initiative The Teenage Pregnancy Prevention Initiative The Violence Prevention Initiative The Work and Health Initiative
Centers for Disease Control and Prevention	
Hogg Foundation for Mental Health	Greater Houston Collaborative for Children
The Robert Wood Johnson Foundation	Allies Against Asthma Fighting Back Initiative, Turning Point Initiative
Kaiser Permanente	Community Health Partnerships
The W. K. Kellogg Foundation	Turning Point Initiative Community Care Network Demonstration Program Community Voices: HealthCare for the Underserved—A National Demonstration of Local Visionary Models Comprehensive Community Health Models of Michigan Initiative

The sources of guidance are growing every day. RAND published a manual on how to hire an empowerment evaluator (Cox et al., 2009). The Group Health Community Foundation (2001) published a guide to improve stakeholder collaboration. The National Service-Learning Clearinghouse[25] provides reference guides and materials concerning community-based work. The Workgroup for Community Health and Development maintains the Community Toolbox,[26] an online resource to facilitate community-based evaluation and empowerment. Similarly, the National Institute of Environmental Health Sciences is drafting an Evaluation Metrics Manual for its Partnerships for Environmental Public Health program.[27] The list is growing every day.

I am not alone in seeing this portrait of the present and this vision of the future. The Aspen Institute Roundtable on Community Change also supports this view of our current state of comprehensive community change and the future. They conducted a review of 48 major comprehensive community initiatives over the past two decades. They see the same expansion of actors, institutions, and opportunities:

> Over the course of the past 10–15 years, the landscape of community change work has grown and diversified in many important and welcome ways. Most significant is that new kinds of public and philanthropic funding have become available, and more institutional actors are taking on this work, including Community Development Financial Institutions (CDFIs), banks, anchor institutions (such as hospitals or universities), and new local family and health conversion foundations. These institutions have expanded the range of connections, leverage, and capacity available to poor communities, and created opportunities for powerful and innovative work going forward. (Kubisch et al., 2010, p. x)

In other words, there is a movement afoot to transform and to improve the human condition, one community at a time, and it includes nonprofits, government agencies, foundations, businesses, hospitals, banks, and academe.

This book is but the tip of an iceberg. The amount of pride, strength, good will, and optimism in this country are enormous. This book represents an attempt to reveal the magnitude of this force to do good, which lies just beneath the surface in each community throughout the United States.[28]

The time is right to launch a public policy debate about our future and what we can do to make that future the best possible world for our children and our children's children. The Digital Village story is one step in the right direction. Collectively these stories represent the path to revitalizing our communities and rejuvenating a nation. This is a race, the clock is ticking, and the real starting line of public debate and dialogue begins here—at the finish line.

NOTES

CHAPTER 1

1. See Kubisch et al. (2010).
2. See Brown (2001); Jahoda (1975); Johnston (1996); and Konstantin (2002).
3. See Ryan (1976).
4. See the Learning for Sustainability site for more information about resilience in evaluation at http://learningforsustainability.net/susdev/resilience.php. See also Neeman (2009) and Reich, Zauta, and Hall (2010) concerning adult resilience.
5. Kelly (2010) provides an excellent example of how evaluation can be used, in this case by the Annie Casey Foundation, in comprehensive and transformative community change.
6. The digital divide refers to the discrepancy between those who have access to technology and the Internet and those who have been left behind, lacking access to this basic and life-sustaining tool. See Hoffman and Novak (1998).
7. See Fetterman and Wandersman (2005, 2007).
8. Empowerment evaluation has been used in Australia, Brazil, Canada, Ethiopia, Finland, Israel, Japan, Mexico, Nepal, New Zealand, South Africa, Spain, and the United Kingdom.
9. See Faber and McCarthy (2005); Korten (2009).
10. Twain (1894), chap. 19, p. 1.
11. See Ryan and Deci (2000).
12. See Bandura (1982) and Martin et al. (2009) for additional discussion about and examples of self-efficacy.
13. See Dawson and Yoong (2010).
14. See the Tuskegee syphilis experiment to provide an insight into the basis for this distrust of legitimate external authorities. Useful readings include Jones (1981) and Katz et al. (2006).
15. See Wellman (2002) for additional information about glocalization.
16. This phrase is in reference to a popular civil rights song and a PBS special highlighting the journey toward social justice.
17. Greene (1977) explains how "social program evaluators are inevitability on somebody's side and not on somebody else's side. The sides chosen by evaluators are most importantly expressed in whose questions are addressed and, therefore, what criteria are used to make judgments about program quality" (p. 25).

CHAPTER 2

1. See Scholten et al. (2006). See also *Stanford Social Innovation Review*, the journal of the Stanford Center on Philanthropy and Civil Society.

2. See House and Price (2009).

3. See also Battelle (2005) concerning the 70/20/10 percent rule, and see Google Culture (2009); Google Management (2009).

4. See also Drucker (2001) concerning the significance of the knowledge worker to organizational productivity.

5. See Packard, Kirby, and Lewis (2006).

6. See Flatte (2006).

7. Tier 1 is a *U.S. News and World Report* classification of top research educational institutions. Stanford University has become popular enough to be mentioned routinely on television shows as the school of choice for the next generation of students.

8. In 2010, Stanford received 32,022 applications and Harvard received 30,489. *New York Times*, August 13, 2010, http://thechoice.blogs.nytimes.com/tag/stanford-university/.

9. Stanford alumni have started many prominent technology companies including Hewlett-Packard (William Hewlett and David Packard), Cisco Systems (Sandra Lerner and Leonard Bosack), Yahoo! (Chih-Yuan Yang and David Filo), Google (Sergey Brin and Lawrence Page), and Sun Microsystems (Vinod Khosla). See Stanford University (2011).

10. See Bielaszka-DuVernay (2008) for a discussion about the dangers of micromanaging.

11. See Institute of Medicine (2010) for recommendations concerning cultivating community buy-in.

12. For additional information about the Haas Center for Community Service, see http://studentaffairs.stanford.edu/haas.

13. Universities appreciate lifelong learning and are committed to investing in the education of one generation after the next. Most universities have a community service obligation and a center or department to help orchestrate this kind of engagement. Stanford's Haas Center is recognized as one of the best and most active models for effective community service delivery in the country, guided by the leadership of Tim Stanton, Nadine Cruz, Leonard Ortolano, and Gabriel Garcia. This model has been adopted in many universities throughout the United States.

14. Fetterman and Wandersman (2005).

CHAPTER 3

1. See Wikipedia for more background information about Carly Fiorina at http://en.wikipedia.org/wiki/Carly_Fiorina. See also Anders (2003) and Fiorina (2006).

2. For additional information about former President Clinton, see Wikipedia at http://en.wikipedia.org/wiki/Bill_Clinton. See also Clinton (2004).

3. For more background information about Reverend Jessie Jackson Sr., see Wikipedia at http://en.wikipedia.org/wiki/Jesse_Jackson.

4. Hewlett-Packard (2000).

5. The Digital Villages also evolved internationally to include Ghana, France, and South Africa. HP Newsroom, October 11, 2001, http://www.hp.com/hpinfo/newsroom/press/2001/011011a.html.

6. For additional information about Reverend Leon Sullivan, a recipient of the Presidential Medal of Freedom, see Sullivan (1998); see also the Sullivan Summit concerning his work in South Africa, http://en.wikipedia.org/wiki/Leon_Sullivan#Leon_H._Sullivan_Summit, and see the PBS special "A Principled Man" (2001) about this civil rights leader.

7. See Smith (2011) and Techme101 (2011) concerning technological tools to help minorities leapfrog across the digital divide.

8. See Bolt and Crawford (2000) and Warschaur (2003) for more detail about the digital divide.

9. Hewlett-Packard (2000).

10. See Horseman (1967) for more information about manifest destiny and Native American policy.

11. See Brown (2001).

12. See web sources for more information about the significance of Alcatraz Island and Native American identify and history at http://www.pbs.org/itvs/alcatrazisnotanisland/nativeland.html.

13. Violent crimes are approximately twice the national average on reservations. See the web news report at http://news.change.org/stories/tackling-crime-on-native-american-reservations. See also Wikipedia concerning conditions such as poverty and alcoholism on the reservation at http://en.wikipedia.org/wiki/Reservation_poverty.

14. Tribal Digital Village's videorecording workshops enabled them to capture their own native history through personal family stories. Technology in this case become a powerful means to an end—cultural preservation and development.

15. For additional information about the network, see http://hpwren.ucsd.edu/.

16. For more information about the Bureau of Indian Affairs, see its website at http://www.bia.gov/WhoWeAre/BIA/index.htm and see Wikipedia at http://en.wikipedia.org/wiki/Bureau_of_Indian_Affairs; see also http://www.answers.com/topic/bureau-of-indian-affairs.

17. See Wikipedia for more demographic information at http://en.wikipedia.org/wiki/East_Palo_Alto,_California.

18. My students raised $10,000 for the Belle Haven School as well. They donated the money in my honor. The money was to be used to help them purchase additional computers. See a news story about my students' donation at http://www.davidfetterman.com/gift.htm.

19. Sharon Williams, interview with the author, East Palo Alto, May 9, 2001.

20. See a brief YouTube video on East Baltimore neighborhoods at http://www.youtube.com/watch?v=D6Q1ZVI27ao.

21. See Wikipedia for more information about Empowerment Zones at http://en.wikipedia.org/wiki/Empowerment_zone.

22. For more information about the Baltimore City Public School System, see its website at http://www.baltimorecityschools.org/site/default.aspx?PageID=1.

23. Hewlett-Packard (2003).

24. Hewlett-Packard (2004).

CHAPTER 4

1. See Fetterman and Bowman (2002).
2. See Cox at el. (2010) concerning CDC's DELTA and EMPOWER programs. See also the CDC guide to hiring an empowerment evaluator (Cox et al., 2009).
3. See examples of empowerment evaluation used in three separate Native American projects at http://www.davidfetterman.com/NativeAmerican.htm.
4. For additional background about measuring empowerment, see Israel et al. (1994); Romero et al. (2006); and Wiggins (2010).
5. Wandersman et al. (2005), p. 28.
6. Novick (1998) presents his view on objectivity as such: "It seems to me that to say of a work of history that it is or isn't objective is to make an empty observation; to say something neither interesting nor useful" (p. 6). See also Greene (1997) concerning evaluation as advocacy.
7. See Fetterman (2004, 2012a) for a more detailed explanation of these theories in relation to empowerment evaluation.
8. One of the goals of the Western Association of Schools and Colleges (an accrediting agency in higher education) is building a culture of evidence; see http://www.wascsenior .org/commission. In addition, this concept can be applied to almost all fields; see Burnaford (2006) for an application to the evaluation of the arts.
9. For more information about the role of the critical friend, see Fetterman (2009); Fetterman, Deitz, and Gesundheit (2010).
10. See Scriven's (1997b) discussion of goal-free evaluation, in which an evaluator never talks to program staff or reads program documents, and Stufflebeam (1994) for the objectivist position. See Fetterman (1995) and Greene (1997) for a discussion about vested interests, subjectivity, and evaluation.
11. See Schön (1987) concerning distinctions between knowing-in-action and reflection-in-action.
12. See Rogoff, Matusov, and White (1998) for more detail about a community of learners. For examples of learning organizations in education, also see Astuto et al. (1993). For more about communities of practice, see Lave and Wenger (1991), as well. As the groups mature and become more specialized (and meet as specialized groups), they evolve into communities of practice.
13. See Argyris and Shön (1978, 1996) and Senge (1990) for more information about learning organizations.
14. See Reason (2008) for more information about reflective practitioners in action research. See also Schön (1988).
15. The empowerment evaluation approach can take a variety of forms, including a ten-step approach developed by Chinman, Imm, and Wandersman (2002).
16. See Fetterman (1996b, 1998) for a discussion about some of the tech tools of the trade used in empowerment evaluation. For more information concerning webpages, collaborative websites, videoconferencing over the net, and blogging in evaluation, see also Fetterman, "CPE Week: David Fetterman on Empowerment Evaluation," at http://aea365 .org/blog/?p=2746.

17. See Argyris and Schön (1978) for a distinction between single and double loop learning in organizations. (Single loop involves identifying an error and a fix to continue present policy and practice. Double loop involves detecting an error and questioning basic assumptions about practice, such that modifications occur that make the organization rethink the status quo; see also Wikipedia at http://en.wikipedia.org/wiki/Organizational_learning.)

18. See Argyris and Schön (1996).

19. See Bohm (1996) for an in-depth discussion about dialogue.

20. Zerubavel (2006) provides a sociological rather than a psychological view of denial.

21. The term "continual" was selected because typically the evaluation process is repeated frequently, as compared with the term "continuous," which actually means uninterrupted.

22. See Deming (1986) concerning a similar conception that focuses on continual quality improvement.

23. See Wang and Ahmed (2003).

24. See Cheadle et al. (1997) for a conference report about integrating the evaluation more closely into program development.

CHAPTER 5

1. See Barrett (2009/2010). For more information about the tribe, see http://www.viejas bandofkumeyaay.org/.

2. See Suarez (2003). For more information about the tribe, see http://www.jamulindian village.com/.

3. See Chappa (1992). For more information about the tribe, see http://www.barona-nsn .gov/index.php?q=home.

4. See Sifuentes (2011) for more information about casino-related concerns characteristic of many reservations. For more information about the tribe, see http://www.kumey aay.info/los_coyotes.html.

5. See McGovern (1995) for the landfill dispute. For more information about the tribe, see http://en.wikipedia.org/wiki/Campo_Indian_Reservation.

6. See Wozencraft (1852) for the tribe's treaty. For more information about the tribe, see http://www.pages.drexel.edu/~kmv32/class/.

7. See Soto (2008) for additional insight into the interwoven nature of tribal life and casinos. For more information about the tribe, see http://en.wikipedia.org/wiki/Manzanita _Band_of_Diegueno_Mission_Indians.

8. See Sifuentes (2008) for more information about the interrelationship between tribal affiliation and casino politics. For more information about the tribe, see http://en.wikipe dia.org/wiki/San_Pasqual_Band_of_Diegueno_Mission_Indians.

9. See Gaughen (2011) for an example of a dispute about garbage dumps and desecrating sacred Pala land. For more information about the tribe, see http://www.palatribe.com/.

10. See PR Newswire (2010) concerning receipt of federal grants toward policing alcohol and substance abuse related incidents. For more information about the tribe and the casino, see http://www.casinopauma.com/tribe.php.

11. See Soto (2010) for tribe's suit against the state concerning casino slot machines. For more information about the tribe within the context of the Kumeyaah Nation, see http://www.kumeyaay.info/.

12. See 10News.com (2011) for another reservation casino related story. For more information about the tribe, see http://www.lajollaindians.com/.

13. See Native American Environmental Protection Coalition (2011) for more information about the tribe from a border perspective. For more information about the tribe, see http://en.wikipedia.org/wiki/Inaja_and_Cosmit_Indian_Reservation.

14. See Gorman (1992) for an example of financial desperation that received national news as the tribe expressed an interest in applying for a nuclear waste dump on the reservation. For more information about the tribe, see http://en.wikipedia.org/wiki/Mesa_Grande_Band_of_Diegueno_Mission_Indians.

15. See Barfield (2007) for background information about the role of the matriarch in the tribe's history. For more information about the tribe, see http://en.wikipedia.org/wiki/La_Posta_Band_of_Diegueno_Mission_Indians.

16. See Soto (2009) for an insight into conflicts concerning casinos, annexing land to expand reservation, and property taxes. For more information about the tribe, see http://en.wikipedia.org/wiki/Sycuan_Band_of_the_Kumeyaay_Nation.

17. See Barfield (2004) for an example of tribal partnerships concerning their casino. For more information about the tribe, see http://en.wikipedia.org/wiki/Ewiiaapaayp_Band_of_Kumeyaay_Indians.

18. For more information about the consortium, see http://www.sctca.net/.

19. For more information about Professor Locklear at Palomar College, see http://daphne.palomar.edu/llocklear/.

20. We used Grove Associates. The graphic art illustrations in this book (Figures 8, 9, and 10) were based on those drawings. However, they were redrawn for publication purposes. For more information about their consulting services, see http://www.grove.com/site/abt_netwrk.html.

21. Muki Hansteen-Izora was a graduate student in the Learning, Design, and Technology program at Stanford University. He was also familiar with our Digital Village partners in East Palo Alto during the evaluation. After the study he became a senior design researcher and strategist with Health Research and Innovation, Intel. For more information about him, see http://www.trilcentre.org/tril-research/people/muki-hansteen-izora.html.

22. Judd Antin was a student of Professor Tony Whitehead at the University of Maryland, College Park. Dr. Whitehead had worked in Baltimore on applied anthropology projects for many years. He provided additional supervision, with me, while Dr. Antin served as an empowerment evaluator. Dr. Antin continued his education at the University of California, Berkeley, where he received his PhD in 2010. His dissertation was titled "Social Operational Information, Competence, and Participation in Online Collective Action."

23. Humor and laughter have been found to be very useful in community-wide initiatives. See the Laughter For A Change website for an example of how it is used when focusing on youth development: http://www.laughterforachange.org/community-initiatives/current-projects/.

CHAPTER 6

1. See Steinberg (1992), and see definition of solidarity at http://www.webref.org/anthro pology/r/rite_of_solidarity.htm.

2. See McMillan and Chavis (1986) for the foundation work in area of building community, and see Walsh (1997) for a discussion about building community by focusing on citizen involvement. See also Boiko-Weyrauch (2011) for the use of technology to promote a sense of community among the Hmong.

3. The expression "keep your eyes on the prize" is based on the title of an influential folk song during the American civil rights movement (Wine, 1965). The reference is no accident in this context. It is a reminder of the undercurrent of social justice in this story. It is the link between the Digital Village as a project and what it came to symbolizes to many members of the Digital Village.

4. See Chambers (1987) for one of the anthropological influences on empowerment evaluation.

5. See Osborn (1963) for principles guiding the application of brainstorming.

6. For more information about Cisco routing and switching training, see http://www .cisco.com/web/learning/le31/le29/learning_recommended_training_routing_switch ing.html.

7. See Pinkett and O'Bryant (2003) concerning building community, empowerment, and self-sufficiency. See Alcantara (2011) and Davis (2011) for examples of urban farms to promote community self-sufficiency.

8. Continuing to grow involves transitional funding from the initial seed money to other grants and related forms of support. Some organizations reach a self-sustaining level of operation sooner than others, based on market conditions, type and quality of service, knowledge of resources available, entrepreneurial capacity, and so on. Few organizations are able to jump immediately from their initial seed money to complete self-sufficiency.

9. The overall average rating across activities was a 5.21 on a 10-point scale. Individual tribal ratings ranged from a 1.7 to an 8 on a 10-point scale. The tribes had excellent visual or photographic evidence to document their successful efforts building networks. In addition, planning documents and dedicated efforts concerning cultural documentation were evidenced, particularly by the local museum.

10. There has been a tremendous amount of speculation about whether this merger was a failure or a success. It had a somewhat disruptive impact on operations in the short run. However, after Hurd succeeded Fiorina and applied his management expertise to it, the merger was reassessed as a success (Rosen, 2008).

11. See Johnson (2010) for a more accurate description of this moment. It is part of a "slow hunch" process in which good ideas emerge over time.

12. Community informatics is central to this discussion as it links technology and communication with community development. See Gurstein (2007).

13. See Brown, Pitt, and Hirota (1999), Hood et al. (1996), and Mettessich and Monsey (1992) for discussions about the importance of collaboration in community-based initiatives.

14. See Green (2003) and Green and Mercer (2001) for an illuminating discussion about the tensions between federal funding initiatives and local concerns.

15. See Chaskin (2011) for a definitional framework for capacity building and case studies. See also Kubisch et al. (2010).

16. See Gray, Duran, and Segal (1997) for a summary of critical characteristics of comprehensive community initiatives, including training, collaboration, capacity building, and finance.

17. The top eleven activities included program development, management (implementation), technology integration and institutionalization, infrastructure development (technology), evaluation, capacity building, training, collaboration, communication (internal and external), client case management, and fund-raising. The overall average across activities was 5.5 on a 10-point scale. Individual ratings were similar with a range of 4.5 to 6.1.

18. Practice should be based on evidence. Evidence should be based on both quantitative and qualitative data. However, there has been an overreliance on statistical significance as compared with systematic, contextualized, and triangulated qualitative data. Moreover, many researchers and evaluators have underestimated what most ethnographers take for granted: the role of context in making meaning. Context is required to meaningfully interpret data, to make sense of everyday life, and to make practice work.

19. The overall average rating across activities was a 3 on a 10-point scale, which highlighted how self-critical and straightforward the groups were concerning their own self-assessment.

CHAPTER 7

1. For more information about theory of change and logic models, see http://learningfor sustainability.net/evaluation/theoryofchange.php.

2. See Donaldson (2003, 2007) and Rogers et al. (2000) for more information about program theory. See also the following websites for more information about assessing program theory: http://mechanisms.org/modules.php?name=Content&pa=showpage&pid=9; http://en.wikipedia.org/wiki/Program_evaluation#Assessing_program_theory.

3. Interventions come in all shapes, sizes, and colors. They range from reading recovery programs (Grehan et al., 2007) to gang intervention programs (Spergel et al., 2002).

4. See Lennihan (2006) for a discussion about funding and sustainability.

5. There is a long history of conflict concerning qualitative versus quantitative paradigms. However, at this time the norm in the field is to combine qualitative and quantitative approaches to produce the most robust results. See Creswell (2009), Ragin (1987), and Tashakkori and Teddlie (1998) for guidelines on how to apply mixed methodologies.

6. See the Centers for Disease Control and Prevention (2008) for guidelines on establishing baselines in tobacco prevention evaluation.

7. See Whitbread (2009) for a design manual for digital printing. This is distinct from digital publishing (Kasdorf, 2003), which focuses on publishing newspapers, magazines, and books using a digital format or medium.

8. See Flickenger (2003) for an introduction to building a wireless community.

9. They secured an E-Rate grant, providing $1 million per year toward building and maintaining the network from the telephone company. (E-Rate is the commonly used name for the Schools and Libraries Program of the Universal Service Fund, which is adminis-

tered by the Universal Service Administrative Company under the direction of the Federal Communications Commission.)

10. See Sunwolf and Frey (2005) concerning advice on how best to facilitate group communication. See also Tannen (1986) for examples of everyday miscommunication.

11. Crisis can be liberating. A facet of empowerment evaluation is liberation. It can set the stage for people to free themselves from pre-existing roles and constraints. See Fetterman (1996a, pp. 16–18) for examples in practice.

12. Statistical significance is an important tool in evaluation. However, there are problems with an excessive reliance on statistical significance: see Hardy and Bryman (2009); Sussman, Steinmetz, and Peterson (1999); and Ziliak and McCloskey (2008). See also Fetterman (1982) concerning the misapplication of the treatment-control design in a national evaluation.

13. For a definition of face validity, see http://www.experiment-resources.com/face-va lidity.html; see also Bornstein (2003).

14. See Fitzpatrick, Sanders, and Worthen (2010) for distinctions between formative and summative evaluation. See also Wikipedia's distinction: "Summative assessment is characterized as assessment *of* learning and is contrasted with formative assessment, which is assessment *for* learning" at http://en.wikipedia.org/wiki/Summative_assessment.

15. For an illustration of the author's own tailspin, see the YouTube video "Honda S2000 Spin with Ferraris at Thunderhill Race Track" at http://www.youtube.com/watch?v=YkX xwea95Ck&feature=mfu_in_order&list=UL.

16. Mason (2003), p. 55.

17. See Argyris and Schön (1996); Senge (1990); Senge et al. (2000); and Torres, Preskill, and Piontek (2005) for more information about organizational learning and evaluation.

CHAPTER 8

1. The pretest and posttest concept is the most typical format used to calculate the difference between two points. However, interpolation is useful as well when it is necessary to construct new data points within a range of known data points (see Abramowitz and Stegun, 1972). A Gaussian process is a nonlinear interpolation tool. Also see Gaussian process regression (Stein, 1999).

2. It is unlicensed because the tribes are part of a sovereign nation and therefore not under the same laws regulating non–Native American life.

3. See Costantino and Greene (2003) and McClintock (2003/2004) for discussions about the use of narratives in evaluation.

4. See Hurworth et al. (2005) for applications of photography in evaluation. See also Torres, Preskill, and Piontek (2005). Schratz-Hadwich, Walker, and Egg (2004) discuss the use of photography as a participatory ethnographic tool.

5. See Nelson (1998) concerning storytelling. Kruger (2010) also provides useful advice concerning the use of stories in evaluation. Boss (2011) provides additional insights into linking stories in the field with funders.

6. See Wang and Burris (1994) for a description of the photo novella that was the origins of Photovoice. Wang and Burris (1997) provide an updated description. Lopez (2010) provides useful insights on the AEA365 blog concerning the use of Photovoice: http://

aea365.org/blog/?tag=photovoice. A visual of the process, called Photovoice Process (Pho-tovoiceHamilton), is available on YouTube (2008) at http://www.youtube.com/watch ?v=shrFa2c305g. The charitable organization called Photovoice applies this tool; see http://www.photovoice.org/.

7. See Banaszewski (2002) for an example in the classroom. See also the Educational Uses of Storytelling home page at http://digitalstorytelling.coe.uh.edu/index.html and the Center for Digital Storytelling at http://www.storycenter.org/index1.html.

8. For more information, see the Center for Digital Storytelling at http://www.storycenter .org and Photovoice at http://www.photovoice.com.

9. See Fetterman (2010) for a detailed discussion about ethnographic methods.

10. For free templates, see http://www.spreadsheetzone.com/?gclid=CM3spNTAxaoCF RxSgwodZEcD1g.

11. S.T. Coleridge (1810) was one of the first to use the expression as an area of weakness, "Ireland, that vulnerable heel of the British Achilles!"

12. In business the deeper the penetration of the market, the higher the volume of sales. This is part of Ansoff's matrix (1957) in business planning for growth.

13. For more information about the Montessori methods, see Montessori (1964).

14. Transformative learning that uses evaluation has many influences including Mezirow's work in adult learning (1997, 2000).

15. See Bonate (2000) for a discussion about pretest and posttest designs.

16. See Ryan (1976) for a detailed description of the "blaming the victim" phenomenon.

CHAPTER 9

1. See Centers for Disease Control and Prevention (2008) for detailed instructions on conducting process evaluations.

2. See Starr et al. (2005) concerning outcome indicators focusing on tobacco prevention programs for additional instruction in this area.

3. For additional discussion about capacity building, see Adams and Dickinson (2010); Compton, Baizerman, and Hueftle-Stockdill (2002); Fetterman and Wandersman (2005); Garcia-Iriate et al. (2011); Preskill and Boyle (2008). Also see Wikipedia at http://en.wiki pedia.org/wiki/Capacity_building.

4. See Maxwell (2008) for an insight guide to mentoring in business and management.

5. See Vygotsky (1978).

6. Experiential learning was developed by scholars such as John Dewey (Dewey, 2009; Kolb and Fry, 1975) and Kurt Lewin (1948). Kolb (1984) helped to further popularize the concept. Itin (1999) has called for a revival of the approach to better prepare for the requirements of the twenty-first century.

7. See Prahalad and Hamel (1990) concerning core competence in business.

8. A supply chain is a system designed to move a product or service from a supplier to a customer. The term also applies to the process involved in transforming a natural resource into a finished product that is delivered to a customer.

9. The ten principles guiding empowerment evaluation are (1) improvement; (2) community ownership; (3) inclusion; (4) democratic participation; (5) social justice; (6) community

knowledge; (7) evidence-based strategies; (8) capacity-building; (9) organizational learning; and (10) accountability. See Fetterman and Wandersman (2005).

10. For additional examples of how to use evaluation to build organizational capacity, see Preskill and Russ-Eft (2005) and Preskill and Torres (1999).

11. Digital photography was used extensively throughout the evaluation. The use of photography was guided by classics in the field of visual anthropology, including Collier and Collier (1986), Heider (2006), and Hockings (2003). See Rosenstein (2000) concerning the use of video for program evaluation. Digital photography also requires software to appropriately crop and to size pictures. Photoshop was used in this evaluation. See Carlson (2011) and Sheppard (2011) for instructions on the use of this software.

12. Videoconferencing was used throughout the evaluation including connecting from my classroom in Wallenberg Hall at Stanford University and the Tribal Digital Village. See Fetterman (1996) for additional information about videoconferencing in educational settings.

13. Digital Village members used Zoomerang and Surveymonkey throughout the evaluation to help determine if specific programs were viewed as working as designed both internally and by the larger community. See Ritter and Sue (2007) for examples and directions concerning the use of online surveys in evaluation.

14. Empowerment evaluation workshops are provided annually at the American Evaluation Association, in addition to organization-specific training workshops.

CHAPTER 10

1. The conventional reference is a return on investment (ROI), in which the return from an investment is divided by the cost. See Friedlob and Plewa (1996) and Phillips (2003) for a variety of applications. An evolving concept in the field is the social return on investment (SROI). It attempts to measure the social and financial value created by a nonprofit. See Elkington and Hartigan (2008) and Surhone, Tennoe, and Henssonow (2010) for a detailed discussion of this concept. It is the term used in Chapter 2 because HP was loosely applying this concept at the beginning of the project. I used the community return on investment (CROI) at the end of the book because it more accurately reflects how value was determined by the end of the effort. It is derived primarily from the community's goals and values instead of an external assessment of the effort or accomplishment.

2. See Camarillo (2007) for a portrait of the new racial frontier in California's minority-majority cities, including East Palo Alto.

3. See Sifuentes (2008) for an example of continuing tribal conflicts. Most contemporary examples focus on casinos.

4. Plato's *Republic* (380 BCE) represents one of the early depictions of a utopian world. The collaboration was not born out of this kind of idealistic dream. In contrast, it focused on vested interests and finding a common denominator across groups.

5. See Crano (1995) and Sivacek and Crano (1982) concerning the role of vested interests in shaping behavior.

6. In another large-scale project with a different funder, which focused on housing, the donor took over the project because members of the community were not getting the homes built fast enough. This was similar to what we experienced in East Palo Alto at

the beginning of this story. When the funder completed the project on budget and on time, they handed the homes over to the community. They looked beautiful. In less than two years, however, the homes were not maintained, in a state of disrepair, and in some cases trashed. Why? There was no ownership and no capacity was built to maintain the homes.

7. Self-determination is the theoretical foundation for empowerment evaluation. It is defined as the ability to chart one's own course in life. My work with self-determined children and young adults with disabilities informs much of my earlier empowerment evaluation work (Fetterman, 1996, pp. 7–8). For additional information about self-determination theory, see Deci and Ryan (1985, 2004). See also Bandura (1982) concerning self-efficacy and Mithaug (1993) concerning self-regulation theory.

8. Empowerment evaluation has been influenced by my work with individuals with disabilities, including individuals with cognitive and physical disabilities, as well as gifted and talented children (with and without physical disabilities) (Fetterman, 1988). Fostering dependency represents another barrier for individuals with disabilities. Rim (2008) explains how dependency factors contribute to the phenomenon of bright children getting poor grades. Drinka (2009) focuses on the thin line between compassionate care and fostering dependency in working with individuals with disabilities.

9. See Sanders (1997) for more information about cluster evaluations.

10. For additional background and discussion about politically correct speech, see Perry (1992) and Schultz (1993).

11. I learned about this path from my coach while on the track in his car as his passenger. He showed me how it was done. I thought he was crazy at first as he cut every corner at breakneck speed and drove on every inch of the road including the "safety" berms on the edges of the road. When we returned to the pit, however, his track time was far ahead of any competitor. He used every inch of the road to cut every corner and every second off his time.

12. See Patton (1997a, 1997b) and Vanderplatt (1995).

13. Klugman's (2010) highlighted values include the following: (1) resources should be distributed so that everyone can live a decent life; (2) human beings all have equal human rights and should be recognized in all of their diversity; (3) all people should be represented and be able to advocate on their own behalf.

14. *Brown v. Board of Education of Topeka*, 347 U.S. 483, May 17, 1954, required desegregation of the public schools.

15. Public Law 88-352 was signed July 2, 1964, by President Johnson.

16. Martin Luther King Jr. delivered the "I Have a Dream" speech at the 1963 Washington, D.C., Civil Rights March.

17. Replication is a biological, not a sociological or an anthropological, concept. The focus of study should be on how social programs adapt to their environment. For additional discussion on this topic concerning a national study of dropout programs, see Fetterman (1981).

18. Community-Campus Partnerships for Health also provides a rich resource of guides and templates for community-based research and evaluation; see http://CES4Health.info/.

19. See Minkler et al. (2003) for an extensive discussion about community-based participatory research and public health funding.

20. According to Devon C. Payne-Sturges, DrPH, assistant center director for Human Health, ORD/ National Center for Environmental Research, "my agency is reorganizing its environmental research to be more community-based and involve stakeholders more in the development of the research questions and conduct of the research." In addition, in line with the U.S. Environmental Protection Agency's Seven Priorities for EPA's Future, the Office of Environmental Justice has created an EPA's Environmental Justice Listserv.

21. The Institute of Translational Health Sciences (http://www.ITHS.org) announced the "availability of research activity grants for community, tribe, or practice-based research. The Community/Practice/Tribe-Based Research Activity Funding Program is sponsored by two ITHS cores: the Center for Scientific Review (CSR) and the Community Outreach and Research Translation (CORT) core. The CORT team supports research partnerships across community and academic settings. Its current focus is developing research networks with American Indian and Alaska Native communities and with primary care clinical practices in the *WWAMI* states (Washington, Wyoming, Alaska, Montana, and Idaho). The goal is to involve communities and practices in every stage of health research and to promote studies that address their priorities and health concerns. CORT also helps them build research capacity by providing research training and experience. This funding program is for community, tribes and practices only. Members of the academic research community are NOT eligible to apply."

22. See Fetterman, Kaftarian, and Wandersman (1996) and W.K. Kellogg Foundation (2009).

23. See Kelly (2010) for five simple rules when evaluating comprehensive community initiatives.

24. Other foundations and their initiatives include the following: the Allina Foundation (Improving Attendance and Participation Among Students with Asthma in the Minneapolis Public Schools); Colorado Trust Teen Pregnancy Prevention (Home Visitation Learning Group); Health Resources and Services Administration (Community Access Program); the Kansas Health Foundation (School and Community Sexual Risk Reduction Replication Initiative); Dorothy Rider Pool Health Care Trusts (Measurable Enhancement of the Status of Health); and the Sierra Health Foundation (Community Partnerships for Healthy Children Initiative).

25. The National Service-Learning Clearinghouse's URL is http://www.servicelearning.org/what-is-service-learning.

26. The URL for the Community Toolbox is http://ctb.ku.edu/en/default.aspx.

27. The draft is available at http://bit.ly/es392n.

28. This book focuses on a large-scale case example in the United States. However, empowerment evaluation is a global phenomenon, including projects in Australia, Brazil, Canada, Ethiopia, Finland, Israel, Japan, Mexico, Nepal, New Zealand, South Africa, Spain, and the United Kingdom.

REFERENCES

Abramowitz, M., and Stegun, I.A., eds. (1972). Interpolation. In *Handbook of Mathematical Functions with Formulas, Graphs, and Mathematical Tables*. New York: Dover, §25.2, pp. 878–882.

Adams, J., and Dickinson, P. (2010). Evaluation Training to Build Capability in the Community and Public Health Workforce. *American Journal of Evaluation*, 31 (September): 421–433.

Alcantara, K. (2011). Bushwick City Farms Promote Community Self-sufficiency. *NS Newsdesk*, June 24. http://newyork.nearsay.com/nyc/williamsburg-greenpoint-bush wick/bushwick-city-farms-masha-radzinsky.

Anders, G. (2003). *Perfect Enough: Carly Fiorina and the Reinvention of Hewlett-Packard*. New York: Portfolio.

Ansoff, H.I. (1957). Strategies for Diversification. *Harvard Business Review*, 35(2):113–124. http://foswiki.org/pub/Sandbox/SimiWiki/Strategies_for_diversification.pdf.

Antin, J. (2005). Empowerment Evaluation: From Theory to Practice. *Practicing Anthropology*, 27(2):23–26.

———. (2010). Social Operational Information, Competence, and Participation in Online Collective Action. PhD diss., University of California, Berkeley.

Argyris, C., and Schön, D.A. (1978). *Organizational Learning*, vol. 1: *A Theory of Action Perspective*. Reading, MA: Addison-Wesley.

———. (1996). *Organizational Learning*, vol. 2: *Theory, Method, and Practice*. Reading, MA: Addison Wesley.

Astuto, T.A., Clark, D.L., Read, A-M., McGree, K., and Fernandez, L. de K.P. (1993). *Challenges to Dominant Assumptions Controlling Educational Reform*. Andover, MA: Regional Laboratory for the Educational Improvement of the Northeast and Islands.

Banaszewski, T. (2002). Digital Storytelling Finds Its Place in the Classroom. *MultiMedia Schools* (January/February). http://www.infotoday.com/MMSchools/jan02/banaszew ski.htm.

Bandura, A. (1982). Self-efficacy Mechanism in Human Agency. *American Psychologist*, 37(2):122–147.

Barfield, C. (2004). Ewiiaapaayp Tribe Betting on Alpine Casino. *San Diego Union-Tribune*, August 20. http://www.signonsandiego.com/uniontrib/20040820/news_7m20casino .html.

———. (2007). Tiny, Remote Tribe in East County Owes Existence to Late Matriarch. *San Diego Union-Tribune*, February 5. http://www.signonsandiego.com/uniontrib/20070205/news_1n5laposta.html.

Barnard, F.R. (1921). One Look Is Worth a Thousand Words. *Printer's Ink*, December 8.

Barrett, B. (2009/2010). The Kumeyaay Way. BWP Media Gaming Group and the Viejas Band of Kumeyaa Indians.

Battelle, J. (2005). Google CEO Eric Schmidt Gives Us His Golden Rules for Managing Innovation. *CNN/Money*, December 1. http://money.cnn.com/magazines/business2/business2_archive/2005/12/01/8364616/index.htm.

Berk, R., and Rossi, P.H. (1976). Doing Good or Worse: Evaluation Research Politically Re-examined. *Social Problems*, 23(3):337–349.

Bielaszka-DuVernay, C. (2008). Micromanage at Your Peril. Harvard Business School. http://blogs.hbr.org/hmu/2008/02/micromanage-at-your-peril.html.

Bohm, D. (1996). *On Dialogue*. London: Routledge.

Boiko-Weyrauch, A. (2011). Teleconferencing Promotes Sense of Community Among Hmong. *Voice of America*, August 8. http://www.voanews.com/english/news/usa/people/Teleconferencing-Promotes-Sense-of-Community-Among-Hmong-125425388.html.

Bolt, D., and Crawford, R. (2000). *Digital Divide: Computers and Our Children's Future*. New York: TV Books.

Bonate, P.L. (2000). *Analysis of Pretest-Posttest Designs*. Boca Raton, FL: Chapman and Hall/CRC.

Bornstein, R. (2003). Face Validity. In M. Lewis-Beck, A. Bryman, and T. Liao, eds., *The SAGE Encyclopedia of Social Science Research Methods*. Thousand Oaks, CA: Sage.

Boss, S. (2011). Amplifying Local Voices: GlobalGiving's Storytelling Project Turns Anecdotes into Useful Data. *Stanford Social Innovation Review* (Summer). http://www.ssireview.org/articles/entry/amplifying_local_voices1/.

Brown, D. (2001). *Bury My Heart at Wounded Knee: An Indian History of the American West*. New York: Owl Books.

Brown, P., Pitt, J., and Hirota, J. (1999). *Collaborative Approaches to Revitalizing Communities*. Chicago: Chapin Hall Center for Children at the University of Chicago.

Bruns, R. (2005). *Jesse Jackson: A Biography*. Westport, CT: Greenwood Press.

Burnaford, G. (2006). *Moving Toward a Culture of Evidence: Documentation and Action Research Inside CAPE Veteran Partnerships*. Veteran Partnerships Report 2005–2006. Chicago: Chicago Arts Partnership in Education. http://www.capeweb.org/wp-content/uploads/2011/05/moving.pdf.

Camarillo, A. (2007). Cities of Color: The New Racial Frontier in California's Minority-Majority Cities. *Pacific Historical Review*, 76(1):1–28.

Carlson, J. (2011). *Photoshop Elements 9 for Mac OS X*. Berkeley, CA: Peachpit Press.

Centers for Disease Control and Prevention. (2008). *Introduction to Process Evaluation in Tobacco Use Prevention and Control*. Atlanta: Centers for Disease Control and Prevention. http://www.cdc.gov/tobacco/publications/index.htm.

Chambers, R. (1987). Shortcut Methods in Social Information Gathering for Rural Development Projects. In *International Conference on Rapid Rural Appraisal*. Khon Kaen, Thailand: University of Khon Kaen, pp. 33–46.

Chappa, C. (1992). *Tribal-State Compact Between the State of California and the Barona Band of Mission Indians.* Washington, DC: Secretary of the Interior. http://www.cgcc.ca.gov/documents/compacts/original_compacts/Barona_Compact.pdf.

Chaskin, R. (2011). Building Community Capacity: A Definitional Framework and Case Studies from a Comprehensive Community Initiative. *Urban Affairs Review,* 47 (July 1): 541–563.

Cheadle, A., Beery, W., Wagner, E., Fawcett, S., Green, L., Moss, D., Plough, A., Wandersman, A., and Woods, I. (1997). Conference Report: Community-Based Health Promotion—State of the Art and Recommendations for the Future. *American Journal of Preventive Medicine,* 13(4):240–243.

Chinman, M., Imm, P., and Wandersman, A. (2002). *Getting to Outcomes 2004.* Santa Monica, CA: RAND Corporation.

Clinton, W. (2004). *My Life.* New York: Knopf.

———. (2005). *My Life: The Presidential Years.* New York: Vintage Books.

Cochrane, A. (1972). *Effectiveness and Efficiency: Random Reflections on Health Services.* London: Nuffield Provincial Hospitals Trust.

Coleridge, T.S. (1810). *The Friend: A Literary, Moral and Political Weekly Paper.* Penrith, UK: J. Brown.

Collier, J., Jr., and Collier, M. (1986). *Visual Anthropology.* Albuquerque: University of New Mexico Press.

Compton, D., Baizerman, M., and Hueftle-Stockdill, S., eds. (2002). *The Art, Craft, and Science of Evaluation Capacity Building.* San Francisco: Jossey-Bass.

Conrad, K.J. (1994). *Critically Evaluating the Role of Experiments.* San Francisco: Jossey-Bass.

Costantino, R.D., and Greene, J.C. (2003). Reflections on the Use of Narrative in Evaluation. *American Journal of Evaluation,* 24(1):35–49.

Cox, P.J., Keener, D., Woodard, T., and Wandersman, A. (2009). *Evaluation for Improvement: A Seven-Step Empowerment Evaluation Approach for Violence Prevention Organizations.* Atlanta: Centers for Disease Control and Prevention.

Cox, P., Ortega, S., Cook-Craig, P., and Conway, P. (2010). Strengthening Systems for the Primary Prevention of Intimate Partner Violence and Sexual Violence: CDC's DELTA and EMPOWER Programs. *Journal of Family Social Work,* 13(4):287–296.

Crano, W.D. (1995). Attitude Strength and Vested Interest. In R.E. Petty and J.A. Krosnick, eds., *Attitude Strength: Antecedents and Consequences.* Mahwah, NJ: Erlbaum, pp. 131–158.

Creswell, J. (2009). *Research Design: Qualitative, Quantitative, and Mixed Methods Approaches.* 3rd ed. Thousand Oaks, CA: Sage.

Csíkszentmihályi, M., Abuhamdeh, S., and Nakamura, J. (2005). Flow. In A.J. Elliot and C.S. Dweck, eds., *Handbook of Competence and Motivation.* New York: Guilford, pp. 598–698.

Daft, R.L. (1989). *Organization Theory and Design.* 3rd ed. New York: West Publishing Company.

Davis, V. (2011). Community Garden Offers Self-sufficiency. *My San Antonio.* http://www.mysanantonio.com/news/local_news/article/Growing-more-comfortable-1014812.php.

Dawson, S., and Yoong, A. (2010). *Alex Yoong: The Driver's Line*. Singapore: Marshall Cavendish.

Deci, E., and Ryan, R. (1985). *Intrinsic Motivation and Self-determination in Human Behavior*. New York: Plenum Press.

———. (2004). *Handbook on Self-determination Research*. Rochester, NY: University of Rochester Press.

Deming, W.E. (1986). *Out of the Crisis*. Cambridge, MA: MIT Press.

Dewey, J. (2009). *Democracy and Education: An Introduction to the Philosophy of Education*. New York: WLC Books. (Original work published in 1916.)

Donaldson, S. (2003). Theory-Driven Program Evaluation in the New Millennium. In S.I. Donaldson and M. Scriven, eds., *Evaluating Social Programs and Problems: Visions for the New Millennium*. The Claremont Symposium on Applied Social Psychology. Mahwah, NJ: Lawrence Erlbaum, pp. 109–141.

———. (2007). *Program Theory–Driven Evaluation Science: Strategies and Applications*. New York: Lawrence Erlbaum.

Drinka, P.J. (2009). Threading the Needle Between Compassionate Care and Fostering Dependency: An Accurate Assessment of Disability. *Journal of the American Medical Directors Association*, 10(2):145.

Drucker, P. (2001). *The Essential Drucker: The Best of Sixty Years of Peter Drucker's Essential Writings on Management*. New York: HarperCollins.

———. (2002). *The Effective Executive*. New York: HarperCollins.

Elkington, J., and Hartigan, P. (2008). *The Power of Unreasonable People: How Social Entrepreneurs Create Markets That Change the World*. Boston: Harvard Business School Press.

Faber, D., and McCarthy, D., eds. (2005). *Foundations for Social Change: Critical Perspectives on Philanthropy and Popular Movements*. Lanham, MD: Rowman & Littlefield.

Fetterman, D.M. (1981). Blaming the Victim: The Problem of Evaluation Design, Federal Involvement, and Reinforcing World Views in Education. *Human Organization*, 40(1):67–77.

———. (1982). Ibsen's Baths: Reactivity and Insensitivity (A Misapplication of the Treatment-Control Design in a National Evaluation). *Educational Evaluation and Policy Analysis*, 4(3):261–279.

———. (1988). *Excellence and Equality: A Qualitatively Different Perspective on Gifted and Talented Education*. Albany: State University of New York Press.

———. (1994). Empowerment Evaluation. *Evaluation Practice*, 15(1):1–15.

———. (1995). In Response to Dr. Daniel Stufflebeam's "Empowerment Evaluation, Objectivist Evaluation, and Evaluation Standards: Where the Future of Evaluation Should Not Go and Where It Needs to Go." *Evaluation Practice*, 16(2):179–199. http://www.davidfetterman.com/InResponseStufflebeam.pdf.

———. (1996a). Empowerment Evaluation: An Introduction to Theory and Practice. In D.M. Fetterman, S. Kaftarian, and A. Wandersman, eds., *Empowerment Evaluation: Knowledge and Tools for Self-assessment and Accountability*. Thousand Oaks, CA: Sage, pp. 3–46.

———. (1996b). Videoconferencing On-line: Enhancing Communication over the Internet. *Educational Researcher*, 25(4):23–27.

———. (1998a). Empowerment Evaluation and the Internet: A Synergistic Relationship. *Current Issues in Education*, 1(4). http://cie.ed.asu/volume1/number4/index.html.

———. (1998b). Webs of Meaning: Computer and Internet Resources for Educational Research and Instruction. *Educational Researcher,* 27(3):22–30.

———. (2001). *Foundations of Empowerment Evaluation.* Thousand Oaks, CA: Sage.

———. (2004). Branching Out or Standing on a Limb: Looking to Our Roots for Insight. In M. Alkin, ed., *Evaluation Roots: Tracing Theorists' Views and Influences.* Thousand Oaks, CA: Sage, pp. 304–318.

———. (2005). Empowerment Evaluation: From the Digital Divide to Academic Distress. In D.M. Fetterman and A. Wandersman, eds., *Empowerment Evaluation Principles in Practice.* New York: Guilford, pp. 92–122.

———. (2009). Empowerment Evaluation at the Stanford University School of Medicine: Using a Critical Friend to Improve the Clerkship Experience. *Ensaio: Avaliacao e Politicas Publicas em Educacao,* 17(63):197–204.

———. (2010). *Ethnography: Step by Step.* 3rd ed. Thousand Oaks, CA: Sage, pp. 83–84.

———. (2012a). Empowerment Evaluation: Learning to Think Like an Evaluator. In M. Alkin, ed., *Evaluation Roots : Tracing Theorists' Views and Influences.* Thousand Oaks, CA: Sage.

———. (2012b). Empowerment Evaluation and Accreditation Case Examples: California Institute of Integral Studies and Stanford University. In C. Secolsky, ed., *Measurement and Evaluation in Higher Education.* London: Routledge.

Fetterman, D.M., and Bowman, C. (2002). Experiential Education and Empowerment Evaluation: Mars Rover Educational Program Case Example. *Journal of Experiential Education.* 25(2):286–295.

Fetterman, D.M., Deitz, J., and Gesundheit, N. (2010). Empowerment evaluation: A Collaborative Approach to Evaluating and Transforming a Medical School Curriculum. *Academic Medicine*, 85(5):813–820.

Fetterman, D.M., Kaftarian, S., and Wandersman, A., eds. (1996). *Empowerment Evaluation: Knowledge and Tools for Self-assessment and Accountability.* Thousand Oaks, CA: Sage.

Fetterman, D.M., and Wandersman, A., eds. (2005). *Empowerment Evaluation Principles in Practice.* New York: Guilford.

———. (2007). Empowerment Evaluation: Yesterday, Today, and Tomorrow. *American Journal of Evaluation*, 28(2):179–198.

Fiorina, C. (2006). *Tough Choices: A Memoir.* New York: Penguin.

Fitzpatrick, J.L., Sanders, J., and Worthen, B. (2010). *Program Evaluation: Alternative Approaches and Practical Guidelines.* 4th ed. New York: Prentice Hall.

Flatte, A. (2006). *Becoming Stanford: The Making of an American University.* Department of Special Collections and University Archives, Stanford University. Videotape.

Flickenger, R. (2003). *Building Wireless Community Networks.* 2nd ed. Sebastopol, CA: O'Reilly Media.

Friedlob, G., and Plewa, F., Jr. (1996). *Understanding Return on Investment: Getting to the Bottom of Your Bottom Line.* New York: Wiley.

Gabbay, J., and LeMay, A. (2011). *Practice-Based Evidence for Healthcare: Clinical Mindliness.* New York: Routledge.

Garcia-Iriate, E., Suarez-Balcazar, Y., Taylor-Ritzler, T., Luna, M. (2011). A Catalyst-for-Change Approach to Evaluation Capacity Building. *American Journal of Evaluation*, 32(2):168–182.

Gaughen, S. (2011). Gregory Canyon Dump Disappoints Pala Tribe. *Temecula Patch*, July 25. http://temecula.patch.com/blog_posts/gregory-canyon-dump-disappoints-pala-tribe.

Gladwell, M. (2008). *Outliers: The Story of Success*. New York: Little, Brown.

Google Culture. (2009). http://www.google.com/corporate/culture.html.

Google Management. (2009). http://www.google.com/corporate/execs.html.

Gorman, T. (1992). Tribe Applies for Nuclear Waste Dump. *Los Angeles Times*, February 15. http://articles.latimes.com/1992-02-15/local/me-1776_1_nuclear-waste.

Gray, B., Duran, A., and Segal, A. (1997). Revisiting the Critical Elements of Comprehensive Community Initiatives. Washington, DC: Office of the Assistant Secretary for Planning and Evaluation, U.S. Department of Health and Human Services.

Green, L.W. (2003). Tracing Federal Support for Participatory Research in Public Health. In M. Minkler and N. Wallerstein, eds., *Community Based Participatory Research for Health*. San Francisco: Jossey-Bass, pp. 410–418.

Green, L.W., and Mercer, S. (2001). Can Public Health Researchers and Agencies Reconcile the Push from Funding Bodies and the Pull from Communities? *American Journal of Public Health*, 91:1926–1929.

Greene, J.C. (1997). Evaluation as Advocacy. *Evaluation Practice*, 18(1):25–35.

Grehan, A., Harrison, L., Ross, S., Nunnery, J., Wohlleb, J., Dejarnette, K., Williams, E., and Dorn, L. (2007). An Evaluation of the Reading Recovery Intervention Program in an At-Risk Urban Setting. Paper presented at the annual meeting of the American Educational Research Association, Chicago, April.

Group Health Community Foundation Evaluation Team. (2001). *Improving Stakeholder Collaboration: A Special Report on the Evaluation of Community-based Health Efforts*. Seattle: Group Health Community Foundation. http://www.cche.org/pubs/ghcf-publication-stakeholder-collaboration.pdf.

Gurstein, M. (2007). *What Is Community Informatics? (And Why Does It Matter)*. Milan: Polimetrica.

Hardy, M., and Bryman, A. (2009). *The Handbook of Data Analysis*. Thousand Oaks, CA: Sage.

Heider, K.G. (2006). *Ethnographic Film*. Austin: University of Texas Press.

Hewlett-Packard. (2000). *The First Three Years 2000–2003: A Community Empowered: Digital Village East Palo Alto* (brochure). Palo Alto, CA: Hewlett-Packard.

———. (2003). *HP's Baltimore Digital Village Celebrates Two Years of Community Collaboration* (brochure). Palo Alto, CA: Hewlett-Packard.

———. (2004). HP Technology Program Advances Education and Economic Development in East Baltimore. News release, June 29. http://www.hp.com/hpinfo/newsroom/press/2004/040629a.html.

Hockings, P., ed. (2003). *Principles of Visual Anthropology*. The Hague: Mouton de Gruyter.

Hoffman, D.L., and Novak, T.P. (1998). Bridging the Racial Divide on the Internet. *Science*, 280 (April 17), 390–391.

Hood, G.E., Hammer, C., Silverman, M., Pearson, L., and Thomas, S. (1996). *Collaboration Works: Communities Tackle Complex Issues* (Special report). Charlottesville, VA: Pew Partnership for Civic Change.

Horseman, R. (1967). *Expansion and American Indian Policy, 1783–1812.* East Lansing: Michigan State University Press.

House, C., and Price, R. (2009). *The HP Phenomenon: Innovation and Business Transformation.* Stanford, CA: Stanford University Press.

House, E. (1980). *Evaluating with Validity.* Thousand Oaks, CA: Sage.

———. (1998). The Issue of Advocacy in Evaluation. *American Journal of Evaluation,* 19(2):233–236.

Hurworth, R., Clark, E. Martin, J., and Thomsen, S. (2005). The Use of Photo-Interviewing: Three Examples from Health Evaluation and Research. *Evaluation Journal of Australasia* 4(1 and 2):52–62.

Institute of Medicine of the National Academies (2010). Community Buy-In. http://www.iom.edu/About-IOM/Making-a-Difference/Community-Outreach/Smart-Bites-Toolkit/Community.aspx.

Israel, B.A., Checkoway, B., Schulz, A., and Zimmerman, M. (1994). Health Education and Community Empowerment: Conceptualizing and Measuring Perceptions of Individual, Organizational, and Community Control. *Health Education Quarterly,* 21(2):149–170.

Itin, C.M. (1999). Reasserting the Philosophy of Experiential Education as a Vehicle for Change in the 21st Century. *Journal of Experiential Education,* 22(2):91–98.

Jahoda, G. (1975). *Trail of Tears: The Story of the American Indian Removal, 1813–1855.* New York: Holt, Rinehart and Winston.

Johnson, R., and Onwegbuzie, A. (2004). Mixed Methods Research: A Research Paradigm Whose Time Has Come. *Educational Researcher,* 33(7):14–26.

Johnson, S. (2010). *Where Good Ideas Come From: The Natural History of Innovation.* New York: Penguin.

Johnston, S. (1996). *The Genocide of Native Americans: A Sociological View.* Hayward, CA: California State University.

Jones, J. (1981). *Bad Blood: The Tuskegee Syphilis Experiment.* New York: Free Press.

Kasdorf, W. (2003). *The Columbia Guide to Digital Publishing.* New York: Columbia University Press.

Katz, R.V., Russell, S.L., Kegeles, S.S., Kressin, N.R., Green, B.L., Wang, M.Q., James, S.A., and Claudio, C.C. (2006). The Tuskeegee Legacy Project: Willingness of Minorities to Participate in Biomedical Research. *Journal of Health Care for the Poor and Underserved* 17(4):698–715.

Kelly, T. (2010). Five Simple Rules for Evaluating Complex Community Initiatives. *Community Investments Online,* 22(1):19–22.

King, Martin Luther, Jr. (1963). "I Have a Dream" speech. March on Washington, Lincoln Memorial, Washington, DC, August 28. http://abcnews.go.com/Politics/martin-luther-kings-speech-dream-full-text/story?id=14358231.

Kirkhart, K. (2010). Eyes on the Prize: Multicultural Validity and Evaluation Theory. *American Journal of Evaluation,* 31(3):400–413.

Klugman, B. (2010). Evaluating Social Justice Advocacy: A Value Based Approach. Washington, DC: Center for Evaluation Innovation. http://evaluationinnovation.org/sites/default/files/Klugman%20Brief.pdf.

Kolb, D.A. (1984). *Experiential Learning. Experience as the Source of Learning and Development.* Englewood Cliffs, NJ: Prentice-Hall.

Kolb, D.A., and Fry, R. (1975). Toward an Applied Theory of Experental Learning. In C. Cooper, ed., *Theories of Group Processes.* London: John Wiley, pp. 33–57.

Konstantin, P. (2002). *This Day in North American Indian History: Events in the History of North America's Native Peoples.* Cambridge, MA: Da Capo Press.

Korten, A.E. (2009). *Change Philanthropy: Candid Stories of Foundations Maximizing Results.* San Francisco: Jossey-Bass.

Krueger, Richard A. (2010). Using Stories in Evaluation. In J. Wholey, K. Hatry, and K. Newcomer, eds., *Handbook of Practical Program Evaluation.* 3rd ed. San Francisco: Jossey-Bass.

Kubisch, A.C., Auspos, P., Brown, P., and Dewar, T. (2010). *Voices from the Field III.* Boulder, CO: Aspen Institute Roundtable on Community Change. http://www.aspeninstitute.org/sites/default/files/content/docs/pubs/VoicesIII_FINAL_0.pdf.

Lave, J., and Wenger, E. (1991). *Situated Learning: Legitimate Peripheral Participation.* Cambridge: Cambridge University Press.

Lennihan, H. (2006). Sustainable Design for Nonprofit Organizations: Finding Funding to Support Sustainability. *Philanthropy News Digest,* March 29. New York: Foundation Center.

Lewin, K. (1948) *Resolving Social Conflicts: Selected Papers on Group Dynamics.* Gertrude W. Lewin, ed. New York: Harper & Row.

Lindstrom, M. (2010a). *Brand Sense.* New York: Simon and Schuster.

———. (2010b). *Buyology.* New York: Doubleday.

———. (2011). *Brandwashed.* Sydney: Random House Australia.

Lopez, K. (2010). Photovoice: Kimberly Kay Lopez on Getting Creative with the Data You Collect and Use for Evaluations! AEA365 A Tip-a-Day by and for Evaluators. August 18. http://aea365.org/blog/?tag=photovoice.

MacDonald, B. (1976). Evaluation and the Control of Education. In D. Tawney, ed., *Curriculum Evaluation Today: Trends and Implications.* London: Macmillan, pp. 125–136.

Martin, M., Catrambone, C.D., Kee, R.A., Evans, A.T., Sharp, L.K., Lyttle, C., Rucker-Whitaker, C., Weiss, K.B., Shannon, J.J., and the Chicago Initiative to Raise Asthma Health Equity Investigative Team. (2009). Improving Asthma Self-efficacy: Developing and Testing a Pilot Community-Based Asthma Intervention for African American Adults. *Journal of Asthma and Clinical Immunology,* 123(1):153–159. doi:10.1016/j.jaci.2008.10.057.

Mason, J.L. (2003). *An Enemy Called Average.* Tulsa, OK: Honor Books.

Maxwell, J. (2008). *Mentoring 101.* Nashville: Thomas Nelson.

McClintock, C. (2003/2004). Using Narrative Methods to Link Program Evaluation and Organizational Development: Reflecting on the Past and Future of Evaluation. Harvard Graduate School of Education, Harvard Family Research Project, 9(4). http://www.hfrp.org/evaluation/the-evaluation-exchange/issue-archive/reflecting-on-the

-past-and-future-of-evaluation/using-narrative-methods-to-link-program-evalua tion-and-organization-development.

McDermott, J., ed. (1981). *The Philosophy of John Dewey*. Chicago: University of Chicago Press.

McGovern, D. (1995). *The Campo Indian Landfill War: The Fight for Gold in California Garbage*. Norman: University of Oklahoma Press.

McMillan, D.W., and Chavis, D.M. (1986). Sense of Community: A Definition and Theory. *Journal of Community Psychology*, 14(1):6–23.

Melnyk, B.M., and Fineout-Overholt, E. (2005). *Making the Case for Evidence-Based Practice*. Philadelphia: Lippincott Williams & Wilkins.

Mettessich, P., and Monseu, B. (1992). *Collaboration: What Makes It Work*. St. Paul, MN: Amherst H. Wilder Foundation.

Mezirow, J. (1997). Transformative Learning: Theory to Practice. In P. Cranton, ed., *Transformative Learning in Action: Insights from Practice*. San Francisco: Jossey-Bass, pp. 5–12.

———. (2000). *Learning as Transformation: Critical Perspectives on a Theory in Progress*. San Francisco: Jossey-Bass.

Minkler, M., Blackwell, A.G., Thompson, M., and Tamir, H. (2003). Community-Based Participatory Research: Implications for Public Health Funding. *American Journal of Public Health*, 93(8):1210–1213.

Mithaug, D.E. (1993). *Self-regulation Theory: How Optimal Adjustment Maximizes Gain*. New York: Praeger.

Montessori, M. (1964). *The Montessori Method*. New York: Schocken Books.

Mubbisher, A. (2011). Engaged IT for the CIO. March 3. http:// mubbisherahmed.word press.com/2011/03/03/eric-schmidt-ex-ceo-and-current-chairman-google-manage ment-style-and-cio/.

Native American Environmental Protection Coalition (2011). *Border 2012: Tribal Accom- plishments and Issues*, no. 6 (May 10–11). http://www.epa.gov/usmexicoborder/docs /tribal/EN-Border2012Final-Wc.pdf.

Neeman, M. (2009). *Developing Resilience: A Cognitive-Behavioural Approach*. New York: Routledge.

Nelson, A. (1998). *Storytelling for Prevention*. Evergreen, CO: WHEEL Council.

Novick, P. (1998). *That Noble Dream: The "Objectivity Question" and the American His- torical Profession*. Cambridge: Cambridge University Press.

Osborn, A.F. (1963). *Applied Imagination: Principles and Procedures of Creative Problem Solving*. 3rd ed. New York: Charles Scribner's Sons.

Packard, D., Kirby, D., and Lewis, K. (2006). *The HP Way: How Bill Hewlett and I Built Our Company*. New York: Collins Paperback.

Patton, M.Q. (1997a). Toward Distinguishing Empowerment Evaluation and Placing It in a Larger Context. *Evaluation Practice*, 18(2):147–163.

———. (1997b). *Utilization-Focused Evaluation: The New Century Text*. 3rd ed. Thousand Oaks, CA: Sage.

Perry, R. (1992). A Short History of the Term "Politically Correct." In P. Aufderheide, ed., *Beyond PC: Toward a Politics of Understanding*. St. Paul, MN: Graywolf Press, pp. 71–79.

Phillips, J. (2003). *Return on Investment in Training and Performance Improvement.* 2nd ed. Burlington, MA: Butterworth-Heinemann, Elsevier Science.

Photovoice Process (2008). Photovoice Hamilton. YouTube. http://www.youtube.com/watch?v=shrFa2c305g.

Pinkett, R., and O'Bryant, R. (2003). Building Community, Empowerment, and Self-sufficiency. *Information, Community, and Society,* 6(2):187–210.

Plato. (380 BCE). *The Republic.* Translated by G.M. Grube. Revised by C. Reeve. Indianapolis, IN: Hackett.

Prahalad, C.K., and Hamel, G. (1990). The Core Competence of the Corporation. *Harvard Business Review,* 68(3):79–91.

Preskill, H., and Boyle, S. (2008). A Multidisciplinary Model of Evaluation Capacity Building. *American Journal of Evaluation,* 29(4):443–459.

Preskill, H., and Russ-Eft, D. (2005). *Building Evaluation Capacity: 72 Activities for Teaching and Training.* Thousand Oaks, CA: Sage.

Preskill, H., and Torres, R. (1999). *Building Capacity for Organizational Learning Through Evaluation.* Thousand Oaks, CA: Sage.

A Principled Man: Reverend Leon Sullivan. (2001). *PBS Picks.* PBS. April 23. http://pbs.org.

PR Newswire (2010). Pauma Tribe to Receive Federal Grant Toward Crime Prevention: Funds Go Toward Policing Alcohol and Substance Abuse Related Incidents. October 12. http://www.prnewswire.com/news-releases/pauma-tribe-to-receive-federal-grant-toward-crime-prevention-104815729.html.

Ragin, C. (1987). *Comparative Methods: Moving Beyond Qualitative and Quantitative Strategies.* Berkeley: University of California Press.

Reason, P. (2008). *Handbook of Action Research: Participative Inquiry and Practice.* 2nd ed. London: Sage.

Reich, J., Zautra, A., and Hall, J.S., eds. (2010). *Handbook on Adult Resilience.* New York: Guilford.

Rim, S. (2008). *Why Bright Kids Get Poor Grades and What You Can Do About It: A Six-Step Program for Parents and Teachers.* 3rd ed. Scottsdale, AZ: Great Potential Press.

Ritter, L., and Sue, V., eds. (2007). *Using Online Surveys in Evaluation.* Berkeley, CA: Jossey-Bass.

Rogers, P., Hacsi, T., Petrosino, A., and Huebner, T. (2000). *Program Theory in Evaluation: Challenges and Opportunities.* San Francisco: Jossey-Bass, p. 87.

Rogoff, B., Matusov, E., White, C. (1998). *Models of Teaching and Learning: Participation in a Community of Learners.* London: Blackwell.

Romero, L., Wallerstein, N., Lucero, J., Fredine, H.G., Keefe, J., and O'Connell, J. (2006). Woman to Woman: Coming Together for Positive Change—Using Empowerment and Popular Education to Prevent HIV in Women. *AIDS Education and Prevention,* 18(5):390–405.

Rosen, B. (2008). The Merger That Worked: Compaq and Hewlett-Packard. *Huffington Post,* April 9. http://www.huffingtonpost.com/ben-rosen/the-merger-that-worked-co_b_95873.html.

Rosenstein, B. (2000). Video Use for Program Evaluation: A Theoretical Perspective. *Studies in Educational Evaluation,* 26(4):373–394.

Ryan, M. (1976). *Blaming the Victim.* New York: Random House.

Ryan, R.M., and Deci, E.L. (2000). Self-determination Theory and the Facilitation of Intrinsic Motivation, Social Development, and Well Being. *American Psychologist,* 55(1):68–78.

Ryan, W. (1976). *Blaming the Victim.* Rev. ed. New York: Random House.

Ryssdal, K. (2009). Eric Schmidt: Interview Transcript. American Public Media, Marketplace World. July 7. http:// www.marketplace.org/topics/world/eric-schmidt-interview -transcript.

Sanders, J.R. (1997). Cluster Evaluation. In E. Chelimsky and W.R. Shadish, eds., *Evaluation for the 21st Century.* Thousand Oaks, CA: Sage, pp. 396–404.

Schmidt, E. (2007). What Is Really Different Now? *New York Times.* December 16. http:// www.nytimes.com/2007/12/16/technology/16ericmemo-web.html?_r=2&oref=slogin &oref=slogin.

Scholten, P., Nicholls, J., Olsen, S., and Galimidi, B. (2006). *SROI: A Guide to Social Return on Investment.* Amstelveen, the Netherlands: Lenthe Publishers.

Schön, D. (1987). *Educating the Reflective Practitioner.* San Francisco: Jossey-Bass.

———. (1988). *The Reflective Practitioner.* San Francisco: Jossey-Bass.

Schratz-Hadwich, B., Walker, R., and Egg, P. (2004). Photo Evaluation: A Participatory Ethnographic Research and Evaluation Tool in Child Care and Education. SOS-Kinderdorf, Hermann Gmeiner Akademe. http://www.aare.edu.au/04pap/sch04245 .pdf.

Schratz-Hurworth, R., Clark, E., Martin, J., and Thompson, S. (2005). The Use of Photo-Interviewing: Three Examples from Health Evaluation and Research. *Evaluation Journal of Australasia,* n.s., 4(1, 2):52–62. http://www.aare.edu.au/04pap/sch04245.pdf.

Schultz, Debra L. (1993). To Reclaim a Legacy of Diversity: Analyzing the "Political Correctness" Debates in Higher Education. New York: National Council for Research on Women. http://www.eric.ed.gov/ERICWebPortal/search/detailmini.jsp?_nfpb=true &_&ERICExtSearch_SearchValue_0=ED364170&ERICExtSearch_SearchType_0=no &accno=ED364170.

Scriven, M. (1997a). Empowerment Evaluation Examined. *Evaluation Practice,* 18(2): 165–175.

———. (1997b). Truth and Objectivity in Evaluation. In E. Chelimsky and W. Shadish, eds., *Evaluation for the 21st Century: A Handbook.* Thousand Oaks, CA: Sage, pp. 477–500.

Senge, P. (1990). *The Fifth Discipline: The Art and Practice of the Learning Organization.* New York: Doubleday/Currency.

Senge, P., Cambron-McCabe, N., Lucas, T., Smith, B., Dutton, J., and Kleiner, A. (2000) *Schools That Learn: A Fifth Discipline Fieldbook for Educators, Parents, and Everyone Who Cares About Education.* New York: Doubleday/Currency.

Sheppard, R. (2011). *Photoshop Elements 9: Top 100 Simplified Tips and Tricks.* New York: Wiley.

Sifuentes, E. (2008). Region: San Pasqual Tribe to Meet on Enrollment Split: Tribal Leaders, Feds to Gather Sunday to Discuss Membership Dispute. *North Country Times,* October 9. http://www.nctimes.com/news/local/sdcounty/article_c6a41d61-236e-5844 -b4d9-76677bca5da7.html.

———. (2011). Barstow City Leaders, Los Coyotes Tribe See Mutual Benefit in Casino. *North Country Times*, July 31. http://www.standupca.org/tribes/Los%20Coyotes%20 Rancheria/barstow-city-leaders-los-coyotes-tribe-see-mutual-benefit-in-casino.

Sivacek, J., and Crano, W.D. (1982). Vested Interest as a Moderator of Attitude Behavior Consistency. *Journal of Personality and Social Psychology*, 43(2):210–221.

Smith, A. (2011). Smartphone Adoption and Usage. Pew Internet and American Life Project. Washington, DC: Pew Research Center. http://pewinternet.org/Reports/2011 /Smartphones.aspx.

Soto, O. (2008). Manzanita Tribe Wants Casino Land as Its Own. *San Diego Union-Tribune*, March 31. http://www.signonsandiego.com/uniontrib/20080331/news_1m31casino .html.

———. (2009). Sycuan Wants Land Added to Reservation. *San Diego Union-Tribune*, June 3. http://www.signonsandiego.com/stories/2009/jun/03/1n3sycuan234550-sycuan-wants -land-added-reservatio/.

———. (2010). Rincon Tribe Wins Slot Suit Against the State. *San Diego Union-Tribune*, March 27. http://www.signonsandiego.com/news/2010/mar/27/rincon-tribe-wins-slot -suit-against-state/.

Spergel, I., Wa, K., Sosa, R., Kane, C., Barrios, E., and Spergel, A. (2002). Evaluation of the Mesa Gang Intervention Program. School of Social Service Administration, University of Chicago. https://www.ncjrs.gov/pdffiles1/nij/grants/209187.pdf.

Stanford University. (2011). Wikipedia, July 20. http://en.wikipedia.org/wiki/Stanford _University.

Stanford University News Service. (1996). Stanford Mourns Loss of David Packard. March 26. http://news.stanford.edu/pr/96/960326packard.html.

Starr, G., Rogers, T., Schooley, M., Porter, S., Wiesen, E., and Jamison, N. (2005). *Key Outcome Indicators for Evaluating Comprehensive Tobacco Control Programs*. Atlanta: Centers for Disease Control and Prevention.

Stein, M.L. (1999). *Interpolation of Spatial Data: Some Theory for Kriging*. New York: Springer.

Steinberg, M. (1992). *Moral Communities: The Culture of Class Relations in the Russian Printing Industry, 1867–1907*. Berkeley: University of California Press, p. 61.

Stephens, B. (2003). *2003 HP Philanthropy and Education Annual Report*. Palo Alto, CA: Hewlett-Packard.

Stufflebeam, D. (1994). Empowerment Evaluation, Objectivist Evaluation, and Evaluation Standards: Where the Future of Evaluation Should Not Go and Where It Needs to Go. *Evaluation Practice*, 15(3):321–338.

Suarez, D.M. (2003). Gambling with Power: Race, Class, and Identity Politics on Indian Lands in Southern California. PhD diss., University of California, Riverside.

Sullivan, L.H. (1998). *Moving Mountains: The Principles and Purposes of Leon Sullivan*. Valley Forge, MA: Judson Press.

Sunwolf, and L.R. Frey. (2005). Facilitating Group Communication. In S.A. Wheelan, ed., *The Handbook of Group Research and Practice*. Thousand Oaks, CA: Sage, pp. 485–510.

Surhone, L., Tennoe, M., and Henssonow, S. (2010). *Social Return on Investment*. Republic of Mauritius: Bestascript.

Sussman, M., Steinmetz, S., and Peterson, G. (1999). *Handbook of Marriage and the Family*. New York: Plenum Press.

Tannen, Deborah. (1986). *That's Not What I Meant!* New York: William Morrow.

Tashakkori, A., and Teddlie, C. (1998). *Mixed Methodology: Combining Qualitative and Quantitative Approaches*. Thousand Oaks, CA: Sage.

Techme101. (2011). Smartphones Are Helping Minorities Leapfrog Over the Digital Divide in the U.S. July 12. http://techme101.com/2011/07/12/smartphones-are-helping-minorities-leapfrog-over-the-digital-divide-in-the-u-s/.

10 News.com. (2011). County Could Be Adding Another Casino: La Jolla Indian Reservation Could Be Home to New Hotel-Casino. February 18. http://www.10news.com/news/26920355/detail.html.

Torres, R., Preskill, H., and Piontek, M. (2005). *Evaluation Strategies for Communication and Reporting: Enhancing Learning in Organizations*. 2nd ed. Thousand Oaks, CA: Sage.

Twain, M. (1894). *The Tragedy of Pudd'nhead Wilson and the Comedy of Those Extraordinary Twins*. Hartford, CT: American.

U.S. Federal Communications Commission. (2003). Meeting of the Advisory Committee on Diversity for Communications in the Digital Age. December 3. http://transition.fcc.gov/DiversityFAC/120309/transcript-120309.doc.

Vanderplatt, M. (1995). Beyond Technique: Issues in Evaluating for Empowerment. *Evaluation*, 1(1):81–96.

Vygotsky, L.S. (1978). *Mind and Society: The Development of Higher Psychological Processes*. Cambridge, MA: Harvard University Press.

Walsh, M. (1997). *Building Citizen Involvement: Strategies for Local Government*. Washington, DC: International City/Council Management Association.

Wandersman, A., Snell-Johns, J., Lentz, B., Fetterman, D.M., Keener, D., Livet, M., Imm, P., and Flaspohler, P. (2005). The Principles of Empowerment Evaluation. In D.M. Fetterman and A. Wandersman, eds., *Empowerment Evaluation Principles in Practice*. New York: Guilford, pp. 27–41.

Wang, C., and Burris, M.A. (1994). Empowerment through Photo Novella: Portraits of Participation. *Health Education and Behavior*, 21(2):171–186. doi:10.1177/109019819402100204.

———. (1997). Photovoice: Concept, Methodology, and Use for Participatory Needs Assessment. *Health Education and Behavior*, 24(3):369–387.

Wang, C.L., and Ahmed, P.K. (2003), Organizational Learning: A Critical Review. *The Learning Organization*, 10(1):8–17.

Warschaur, M. (2003). *Technology and Social Inclusion: Rethinking the Digital Divide*. Cambridge, MA: MIT Press.

Weissbourd, R. (2010). Lessons from the Field: How 21st Century Community Development Can Inform Federal Policy. *Journal of the Institute for Comprehensive Community Development*, Inaugural Issue (December): 8–13.

Wellman, B. (2002). Little Boxes, Glocalization, and Networked Individualism. In M. Tanabe, P. van den Besselaar, and T. Ishida, eds., *Digital Cities II: Computational and Sociological Approaches*. Berlin: Springer-Verlag, pp. 11–25.

Whitbread, D. (2009). *The Design Manual*. Sydney: University of South Wales Press. http://books.google.com/books?id=gvPx-_CjFaIC&pg=PA312&dq=%22digital+printing%22&hl=en&ei=FkyBTMX0AoOKlwfB3u3RDg&sa=X&oi=book_result&ct=result&resnum=3&ved=0CD0Q6AEwAjgU#v=onepage&q=%22digital%20printing%22&f=false.

Whitmore, E., Guijt, I., Mertens, D.M., Imm, P., Chinman, M., and Wandersman, A. (2006). Embedding Improvements, Lived Experience, and Social Justice in Evaluation Practice. In I.F. Shaw, J.C. Greene, and M. Mark, eds., *The SAGE Handbook of Evaluation*. Thousand Oaks, CA: Sage, pp. 340–359.

Wiggins, N. (2010). *La Palabra es Salud*: A Comparative Study of the Effectiveness of Popular Education vs. Traditional Education for Enhancing Health Knowledge and Skills and Increasing Empowerment Among Parish-Based Community Health Workers (CHWs). PhD diss., Portland State University.

Wine, A. (1965). Keep Your Eyes on the Prize. Produced by Reggie and Kim Harris/Brooky Bear Music, 1997.

W.K. Kellogg Foundation (2009). *W.K. Kellogg Foundation Evaluation Handbook*. Battle Creek, MI: W.K. Kellogg Foundation.

Wozencraft, O.M. (1852). Treaty with the Dieguinos. Reprinted in C. Kappler (1929). *Indian Affairs: Laws and Treaties*. Washington, DC: Government Printing Office. http://www.kumeyaay.info/history/Santa_Ysabel_Treaty_1852.pdf.

Zerubavel, E. (2006). *The Elephant in the Room: Silence and Denial in Everyday Life*. New York: Oxford University Press.

Ziliak, S., and McCloskey, D. (2008). *The Cult of Statistical Significance: How the Standard Error Cost Us Jobs, Justice, and Lives*. Ann Arbor: University of Michigan Press.

INDEX